B Cullen
ahir, Rana,
ountee Cullen : poet /
45.64

ARTISTS OF THE HARLEM RENAISSANCE

COUNTEE CULLEN

POET

RANA TAHIR

Cavendish
Square

New York

Published in 2017 by Cavendish Square Publishing, LLC
243 5th Avenue, Suite 136, New York, NY 10016

Copyright © 2017 by Cavendish Square Publishing, LLC

First Edition

Library of Congress Cataloging-in-Publication Data

Names: Tahir, Rana.
Title: Countee Cullen : poet / Rana Tahir.
Description: New York: Cavendish Square Publishing, 2016. | Series: Artists of the Harlem Renaissance | Includes bibliographical references and index. Identifiers: LCCN 2015035471 | ISBN 9781502610683 (library bound) | ISBN 9781502610690 (ebook)
Subjects: LCSH: Cullen, Countee, 1903-1946—Juvenile literature. | Poets, American—20th century–Biography–Juvenile literature. | African American poets—Biography–Juvenile literature.
Classification: LCC PS3505.U287 Z885 2016 | DDC 811/.52–dc23
LC record available at http://lccn.loc.gov/2015035471

Editorial Director: David McNamara
Editor: Amy Hayes/Jill Sherman
Copy Editor: Nathan Heidelberger
Art Director: Jeffrey Talbot
Designer: Stephanie Flecha
Production Assistant: Karol Szymczuk
Production Editor: Renni Johnson
Photo Research: J8 Media

TABLE OF CONTENTS

The Life of Countee Cullen

"But a plea, that upward to Heaven
   he flings—
I know why the caged bird sings!"

—Paul Laurence Dunbar, *Sympathy*

I HAVE A RENDEZVOUS WITH LIFE

Countee Cullen did not just live in interesting times, he curated them. The Harlem Renaissance's unofficial poet laureate had worked tirelessly to ensure that he, and other emerging poets of color, had a place in the American literary landscape. From immensely humble beginnings, his drive and passion brought forth an acclaimed star that burned too brightly and quickly for those who basked in his light.

EARLY LIFE

Very little is known about Countee Cullen's early life. Cullen left no written account of his life. Record keeping at this time was spotty. Most of what we know is based on the stories that his second wife, Ida, and his close friends have told. However, Cullen's stories often proved to be false. He told different versions of his upbringing, which happened in different places depending on

Opposite: Harlem had one of the most condensed populations of blacks at the time of its Renaissance. Here, two children read a history book outside in 1933.

whom you ask. His secrecy about his past leaves much to the imagination. However, school records and United States census data help. Researchers look at all these pieces to put together a clearer picture of Cullen's early years.

According to Ida, Cullen was probably born in Louisville, Kentucky, on May 30, 1903, to Elizabeth Lucas. His name at birth was Countee L. Porter. His New York University registration form also lists his place of birth as Louisville. But his life in Louisville would always remain a mystery. He often changed the story of his early life. He would sometimes claim to have been born in New York. It was also rumored he was born in Baltimore, Maryland, like the Reverend Frederick Cullen, who would later adopt him.

According to census data, when Countee Cullen was eight years old, he was sent to live in New York with his grandmother, Amanda. She lived with John Henry Porter, who was most likely Cullen's grandfather. The reason for the move is unknown. However, researchers speculate that Cullen may have been born out of wedlock. If that were the case, his mother wouldn't have had much help caring for a young child. It would be easier to send him to live with relatives in New York.

Also according to the census, John Henry Porter worked in the theater. However, his specific job is unlisted. He may have worked as a doorman or a porter, according to some accounts. Often the family moved from home to home. As Cullen's future widow would claim, they lived in relative poverty. Moving often also meant that Cullen changed schools many times.

Cullen was, despite these hardships, a brilliant student. Steadfast in his studies, he was known by his peers to be exceptionally smart, with a talent for learning. He attended the Salem Methodist Episcopal Church regularly. He even took part in church programs, such as the Epworth League Sunday evening programs and Sunday school. The Salem Methodist Episcopal Church was the largest congregation in Harlem. At the time, it was run by Reverend Frederick Asbury Cullen.

Newly arrived from the South, this family came to Chicago looking for new opportunities.

Misfortune soon hit Cullen. When he was just fourteen years old, in 1917, his caretaker John Henry died of pneumonia. Porter was fifty-two years old. Almost one year later, his grandmother fell ill. He spent much of his time visiting the hospital, trying to keep her comfortable. Eventually, she passed away, leaving him on his own. It was then that James Gowin, an officer of the church and a friend of Reverend Cullen, approached the reverend in concern for young Countee.

Gowin admired the boy's tenderness and intelligence. He believed Countee deserved an education, but he could not afford to give him one. The reverend, however, could possibly do so with support from the church. Dr. Cullen listened to his friend's proposal. Shortly after, he arranged a meeting with this exceptional student. Both the reverend and his wife, Carolyn, were taken with Countee. They eagerly welcomed him into their home.

THE TURN OF THE CENTURY

At the turn of the nineteenth century, society changed rapidly. Within the last one hundred years, the nation had split from its rural roots. The future of America would be born in the cities.

The end of the **Reconstruction Era** (about 1877) had ended slavery in name only. The South reestablished its plantations. Workers would have to be paid for their work. Plantation owners, however, had not changed their attitudes toward the black people looking for paid work in the fields. Workers remained in near slave-like conditions. The plantation owners continued to profit off cheap labor. Meanwhile, a second **Industrial Revolution** had broken ground. More people were aware of the importance of factories in the new America. Factory jobs had the promise of bringing economic power and new jobs to the North.

An influx of black people moved into major cities like Chicago and New York. They were looking for work and freedom. From 1910 to 1920, in what was called the **Great Migration**, some 5 percent of the black population had moved from the South to the North in search of jobs and a better life. City living did not always bring the promised futures many black people hoped for, but there was more freedom in the North than what was offered in the **Jim Crow** South. As years passed, groups such as the Ku Klux Klan saw a revival in the South, and discrimination was still prevalent throughout the United States.

Countee's life with the Cullens is not well documented. It is clear, however, that he grew to think of the Cullens as his parents. He even took their last name. Despite the close relationship, he felt indebted to their kindness. The feeling of obligation toward them pushed him to work hard. It also tied him to their expectations, for better or worse.

THE CULLENS

When Cullen was not yet fourteen years old, the United States entered World War I. President Woodrow Wilson occupied the Oval Office. Wilson, a Virginian, had idealistic notions for foreign policy, but he promoted racist policies at home. He believed in segregating the federal government. Though he was a leader of the Progressive movement, the name was a misnomer. Non-white Americans saw little change. They knew that the politicians who courted their votes would not support them in policies.

Cullen was coming of age in a time of great upheaval for the American public. The promise of a better future for blacks clashed with old values. Even in his own household, Cullen saw the struggles black people faced nationwide.

Reverend Cullen was a distinguished man. He was admired both for his service to the clergy and for his activism. He had walked a hard road growing up. His parents were former slaves, and when he was two months old, his father died. Frederick was the youngest of eleven children and was raised by a single mother. He grew up in the racially charged atmosphere of Maryland. Frederick lived in poverty, wearing his sisters' clothes as hand-me-downs. The only employment he could find was household work in the homes of well-off white families.

Luckily, his work allowed time for school. Frederick Cullen attended Maryland State Normal School (now Townson University). Eventually, he gained enough schooling to teach in a Baltimore public school. In September 1894, Frederick Cullen attended a

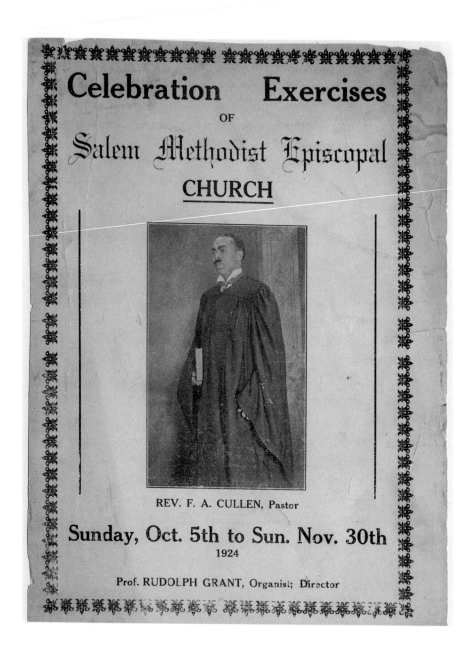

Celebration   Exercises

OF

𝕾𝖆𝖑𝖊𝖒 𝕸𝖊𝖙𝖍𝖔𝖉𝖎𝖘𝖙 𝕰𝖕𝖎𝖘𝖈𝖔𝖕𝖆𝖑

CHURCH

REV. F. A. CULLEN, Pastor

Sunday, Oct. 5th to Sun. Nov. 30th

1924

Prof. RUDOLPH GRANT, Organist; Director

Reverend Cullen's Harlem congregation had started as a small storefront mission. With active recruiting and the influx of migrants, it grew into a large congregation. Here he is featured on a church program.

revival meeting. There, he had a religious awakening. He returned to his hometown of Fairmont, Maryland, to teach but found it difficult to get the resources he needed. Jim Crow laws left black schools ill equipped to provide a meaningful education. Eventually, he left teaching, feeling he could be more of a service to people as part of the church. He attended Morgan College (now Morgan State University) to earn his degree in theology.

In 1900, six years after making the commitment to his faith, he was ordained. He spent two years in Baltimore going back and forth, working at two different churches. After finding success there, he was appointed to Saint Mark's Methodist Episcopal Church in New York City. He worked in the church's storefront mission. There, he provided youth outreach and programs to attract more adult churchgoers. Growing the church's congregation led to his mission becoming an independent church in 1908. Steadily, it became the largest one in Harlem. While on vacation in Atlantic City, Cullen met Carolyn Belle Mitchell. She was a singer and pianist from Baltimore. After a brief courtship, they married and she returned with him to Harlem.

Reverend Cullen knew firsthand how poverty and racism affected black families. It made him an outspoken leader in Harlem. He organized marches and other protest activities. Eventually, he became president of the Harlem branch for the **National Association for the Advancement of Colored People** (NAACP). In addition to his growing role in the community, Reverend Cullen was constantly growing his church. It would eventually become the largest congregation in Harlem. While black Harlem was home to Muslims, Jews, and other faiths, Christianity was a large part of Harlem life. In his home, stories of injustices against black people were discussed and actions were planned. The reverend's young adopted son bore witness to this fervent activism.

Stories of lynchings and people being burned alive traveled quickly. Black people were an easy target of punishment for any perceived slight against whites. A black man who smiled at a white woman could be taken to task for "not knowing his place." Black people accused of a crime had little hope of proving their innocence at trial. Mobs of whites judged them guilty of being colored. Death sentences were dispensed without trial and without fear that the police would interfere. In some cases, white children were taken to witness the lynchings, as though they were for amusement.

When black soldiers of Camp Logan in Houston, Texas, were accused of rioting in a white town, some were hanged without trial. Reverend Cullen took immediate action. He and his committee sent a delegation to see President Wilson about the crisis. James Weldon Johnson was elected the spokesman for the group. They spent a half hour with the president. Eventually, the remaining soldiers were granted clemency by executive order. Their death sentences were changed to life sentences.

The victories were hard fought, but too few. Hearing lynching stories made young Countee feel ill. Later, in a letter to his white school friend William Fuller Brown Jr., Countee admitted that he had once hated all white people. Though that later changed, he was deeply affected by the racism he saw every day.

While the reverend was a civic influence for Countee, his artistry came mainly from the reverend's wife, Carolyn. Known for her lovely voice and skillful piano playing, she taught Countee music. He took it up earnestly. He always credited her musical influence as a gateway into poetry. Poetry was his way of bringing music to the world.

FINDING POETRY

Despite the turmoil around him, Countee was a bright student. In elementary school, he wrote poetry and won several poetry contests. His true blossoming as a poet did not occur until his later school years, though.

Countee's high school days seemed full of joy and promise. He initially attended Townsend Harris Hall High School but then transferred to DeWitt Clinton High School. While there, Mr. George Cronyn, an English teacher, published one of Countee's writing exercises. It appeared in the educational magazine *Modern School*. The poem was titled "To a Swimmer," and it was held up as an example of artistic skill in young people.

The poem was the only **free verse** he would ever publish. It hints at a love or admiration unspoken, and a hope that the swimmer's heart is as true as his or her arms. The tension between what is said and what is unsaid heightens the poem. It creates an inner conflict that is palpable. This silent or unrequited love would be a lifelong **theme** in his work.

With that first poem published, Cullen was faced with an exciting idea: it might be possible to become a full-time poet rather than pursuing poetry as a hobby. Now he was getting praise for his writing. Though it was the admiration of an educational magazine, it was still a valued compliment.

BLACK AMERICA IN 1918

In 1918, Countee took Cullen as his last name. The same year marked a major change for the United States: World War I had ended. Black soldiers returned from war, excited for the new life they had earned on the battlefield. After being treated as heroes in Europe, they expected even greater honors at home. Though black soldiers played important roles in the war abroad, they saw little to no change at home in the United States. Segregation was still the law. It was as if their sacrifices in the war did not matter at all.

The soldiers, heralded as heroes in Europe, were reduced to less than human in Jim Crow America. All around the country, black people were being mistreated and insulted. White people feared the large number of back people moving to urban areas. They

THE SHAME OF AMERICA

Do you know that the United States is the Only Land on Earth where human beings are BURNED AT THE STAKE?

In Four Years, 1918-1921, Twenty-Eight People Were Publicly
BURNED BY AMERICAN MOBS

3436 People Lynched 1889 to 1922

For What Crimes Have Mobs Nullified Government and Inflicted the Death Penalty?

The Alleged Crime	The Victims	Why Some Mob Victims Died:
Murder	1266	Not Turning out of road for white boy in auto
Rape	571	Being a relative of a person who was lynched
Crimes against the Person	615	Jumping a labor contract
Crimes against Property	333	Being a member of the Non-Partisan League
Miscellaneous Crimes	463	"Talking back" to a white man
Absence of Crime	178	"Insulting" white man.
	3436	

Is Rape the "Cause" of Lynching?

Of 3,436 people murdered by mobs in our country, only 571, or less than 17 per cent., were even accused of the crime of rape.

83 WOMEN HAVE BEEN LYNCHED IN THE UNITED STATES

Do lynchers maintain that they were lynched for "the usual crime"?

AND THE LYNCHERS GO UNPUNISHED

THE REMEDY

The Dyer Anti-Lynching Bill Is Now Before the United States Senate

The Dyer Anti-Lynching Bill was passed on January 26, 1922, by a vote of 230 to 119 in the House of Representatives

The Dyer Anti-Lynching Bill Provides:
That culpable State officers and mobsists shall be tried in Federal Courts on failure of State courts to act, and that a county in which a lynching occurs shall be fined $10,000, recoverable in a Federal Court.

The Principal Question Raised Against the Bill is upon the Ground of Constitutionality.

The Constitutionality of the Dyer Bill Has Been Affirmed by—
The Judiciary Committee of the House of Representatives
The Judiciary Committee of the Senate
The United States Attorney General, legal adviser of Congress
Judge Guy D. Goff, of the Department of Justice

The Senate has been petitioned to pass the Dyer Bill by—
28 Lawyers and Jurists, including two former Attorneys General of the United States
19 State Supreme Court Justices
24 State Governors
3 Archbishops, 83 bishops and prominent churchmen
29 Mayors of large cities, north and south.

The American Bar Association at its meeting in San Francisco, August 5, 1922, adopted a resolution asking for further legislation by Congress to punish and prevent lynching and mob violence.

Fifteen State Conventions of 1922 (2 of them Democratic) have inserted in their party platforms a demand for national action to stamp out lynchings.

The Dyer Anti-Lynching Bill is not intended to protect the guilty, but to ensure to every person accused of crime a fair trial by due process of law.

THE DYER ANTI-LYNCHING BILL IS NOW BEFORE THE SENATE
TELEGRAPH YOUR SENATORS TODAY YOU WANT IT ENACTED

If you want to help the organization which has brought to light the facts about lynching, the organization which is fighting for 100 per cent. Americanism, not for some of the people some of the time, but for all of the people, white or black, all of the time?

Send your check to J. E. SPINGARN, Treasurer of the

NATIONAL ASSOCIATION FOR THE ADVANCEMENT OF COLORED PEOPLE
70 FIFTH AVENUE, NEW YORK CITY

THIS ADVERTISEMENT IS PAID FOR IN PART BY THE ANTI-LYNCHING CRUSADERS.

This advertisement for the Dyer anti-lynching bill calls lynching the shame of America. Despite the active campaigning, enough Southern Democrats pushed the bill aside.

wanted to keep the new opportunities and jobs for themselves. Black soldiers, having gotten used to European standards of treatment, were also seen as too uppity by white people. Their confidence enraged racists, particularly in the South. They saw armed black men as threats to their lives. White people were able to discriminate and kill black people without fear that they would go to jail. Even when the offender could be identified, there would be no recourse. Black families were threatened into silence.

Also that year, Republican representative Leonidas C. Dyer introduced an anti-lynching bill to Congress, but the bill would never become law. Southern Democratic senators blocked passage. It seemed like nothing could end black people's suffering.

Meanwhile, Marcus Garvey was preaching a return to Africa. Around the country, he argued for the building of a great black nation. Given the great injustices black people faced, the idea gained some support. He encouraged his supporters to don Pan-African colors and take African or Arab names. They raised money to purchase a fleet of ships that would take them to an idealized Africa and allow them to live with dignity. The talk of Africa and an African heritage pervaded imaginations for decades afterward. Cullen would grapple with popular American ideas of Africa in his future poetry.

DEWITT CLINTON HIGH SCHOOL

In February of 1918, Cullen enrolled in DeWitt Clinton High School. It was a prestigious all boys' school, which would produce a long list of notable alumni: Ralph Lauren, James Baldwin, and Tracy Morgan, to name a few. In 1918, Cullen and his classmates erupted in glee at the end of the Great War. They all looked forward to a new time of prosperity and peace. For Cullen, the joy of the times was likely improved by the recognition he received for his poetry.

Cullen was one of the only black students at his new school, and he felt pressure to prove himself. Though he was not shy about his talent, he was also keenly aware of the place his racial identity set for him. He understood the way his race set him apart from his classmates. Almost every day, he left his black neighborhood to go to his white school. Though neither place was formally segregated, Cullen knew that in effect, both places were. This de facto segregation created a rift, and Cullen's art would straddle these two separate and distinct worlds.

At Clinton, as the students called it, Cullen earned the nickname "Tay." His peers often pronounced his name incorrectly. When they said "Coun-tee," he fired back, "Coun-tay." Cullen was as studious as ever. He volunteered to help fellow students with their Latin in an afterschool tutoring program. He also published poems in the student magazine, *Magpie*.

His first poem of considerable recognition was "I Have a Rendezvous with Life." It was a response to poet Alan Seeger's "I Have a Rendezvous with Death." Seeger had been a soldier in World War I and a member of the French Foreign Legion. Seeger wrote his poem at the front lines, and he was killed in battle in 1916. Two years later, Cullen, moved by this poem, had to respond. He entered his poem in a contest held by the Empire Federation Women's Club and won first place. The organization named him New York's best young poet.

The poem was characteristic of Cullen's poetic aesthetic. He follows a strict **meter** and end rhymes. In addition to its concern with the larger themes of life and death, the poem shows surprising maturity because of its reference to Seeger's work.

Learning from other writers, Cullen taught himself through imitation and by writing reviews. "Facultywocky," a satirical poem about the Clinton faculty, was mirrored off Lewis Carrol's "Jabberwocky." He also reviewed *The Three Mulla-Mulgars* by Walter de la Mare. His short story "Frenchman's Bath" was published. Still inspired by Carolyn's musical talent, he wrote song lyrics.

In 1921, Cullen had the chance to read an original poem in front of a great assembly celebrating President Lincoln's birthday. The poem, "In Memory of Lincoln," was a eulogy for the long-deceased president from the point of view of a black American. The poem was profound in its use of a black man representing the universal man.

Following his successes, Cullen joined *Magpie* on the editorial staff. His reputation preceded him. He earned the admiration and respect of his peers and teachers. By the end of his high school

Alan Seeger, pictured here years before his fateful poem, would inspire a young Cullen to write his own poem about life.

career, Cullen was the associate editor of *Magpie* and editor-in-chief of the *Clinton News*. He was also vice president of student government, president of the Arista Society, chairman of the Senior Publications Committee, and treasurer of the Inter-High School Poetry Association. He won the Regents Scholarship, for which he had taken special classes and tests in many subjects. The scholarship would lessen his college expenses.

Applying to college was an exciting time. After looking at his options and filling out the applications came the waiting. He had his heart set on Columbia University, but his hopes were dashed. He was granted admission, but Columbia would not provide financial aid.

Despite the setback, Cullen continued to excel in all his pursuits. He had another opportunity to speak in front of a large audience. This time he was a finalist for an oratory competition. His subject was "God and the Negro." The 250-word speech gave an overview of black history to present day. He rejected expatriation to Africa, affirmed the existence of a distinctly black identity, and surmised that black people would not be content without equal rights. Their ally in this struggle would be the Almighty, by whatever name one would call Him. He won a gold medal for his speech. The themes, like character over color, spiritual struggle, and the image of Africa, would abound in his future work.

In January 1922, Cullen was chosen as the class poet for graduation. He was to present a poem of his own for the occasion. In October, *Crisis*, the official magazine of the NAACP headed by W. E. B. Du Bois, mentioned Cullen as part of a feature of promising black artists.

The successful past gave way to a now promising future as Cullen enrolled as a freshman in New York University later that year.

ONLY THE BEGINNING

Cullen's life would be defined by his hard work. Carrying with him a deep sense of responsibility and gratitude to his foster parents, he would work tirelessly not just to excel in the realm of writing, which he loved, but also to be a model son.

His success in writing brought him great joy but also more issues, as his writing drew from his experience at a majority white school and his influences were mostly white poets.

In what would seem like little to no time at all, Cullen's star would shine and skyrocket upward. Publishing his first book would bring him to the attention of many prominent figures who

In this photo, taken sometime in the 1930s, Cullen presents himself respectably, dressed in a jacket and tie.

would try to influence him or mold him into their ideals. The Harlem Renaissance would galvanize the country with new young artists, with whom Cullen would form lasting friendships, and conflicts. He would be thrust into the spotlight at a young age as he tried to grapple with questions of who he was and what his place in the world was.

CHAPTER TWO

THE SHROUD OF COLOR

Cullen approached the halls of New York University with the same agility he had at Clinton. In addition to literature, he studied French, Latin, Greek, German, philosophy, and education studies. Taking classes with Hyder E. Rollins, Cullen discovered medieval poetry and the **Romantic** poet John Keats.

Cullen had many literary influences before Keats. One in particular was poet Paul Laurence Dunbar. Cullen felt a strong connection to Dunbar, calling him his brother, both in heart—their poetic vocation—and by blood—their race. Dunbar was one of the first black poets to gain white favor, writing mostly in dialect. His poetry and person gave Cullen, and many others, an image of what was possible for a poet of color.

Keats affected Cullen differently. His poetry had a musical quality that inspired Cullen. For ill or good, Cullen's poetry would be compared to Keats for decades. Another influence was Edna St. Vincent Millay, the first woman to win a Pulitzer Prize in poetry. Cullen wrote his senior thesis on her work.

Opposite: In the 1920s, numerous opportunities would open up for Cullen, among them the doors to the prestigious Harvard University. Here is a photo of Harvard Union.

Cullen continued to work on his poetry and submit to magazines. One poem in particular, "Ballad of the Brown Girl," drew special notice. Cullen's take on a ballad set in Kentucky, it depicted a doomed love triangle. The poem won second prize in the Witter Bynner undergraduate poetry contest. Its publication also won him Witter Bynner's personal friendship. Cullen also had his poem "To a Brown Boy" published in *Bookman*.

Cullen went through major changes during his college years—some artistic and others personal. In 1923, his sophomore year, Cullen started spending time with Nina Yolande Du Bois. She went by her middle name, Yolande, because she was named after her mother, Nina Du Bois. Yolande was the only child of W. E. B. Du Bois, the famous journalist and civil rights activist. The Cullens and the Du Boises were already close family friends. They knew each other through their civil rights activism. W. E. B. Du Bois and Reverend Cullen had worked together on the Camp Logan committee to see President Wilson.

Yolande was studying at Fisk University in Nashville, Tennessee, following in her father's footsteps. She was bright and interested in teaching. However, in her youth she was often ill and needed frequent rest even while in college. Her family connections made her one of the most eligible young women of the time.

When she and Cullen started dating, both continued to see other people. Yolande had a relationship with the jazz bandleader Jimmie Lunceford. Her father did not approve of jazzmen. Cullen was a better suitor, in her father's view. It was clear to the elder Du Bois that Cullen was going somewhere. He was well mannered and part of the **Talented Tenth**, an elite class of educated blacks.

In 1924, his junior year, Cullen won honorable mention in the Witter Bynner Poetry Contest for the poem "Spirit Birth." His poem "Simon the Cyrenian Speaks" was published in *Poetry* magazine, one of the country's most prestigious poetry publications. Three poetic epitaphs were published as well; more were accepted in *Century, Harper's, Bookman, American Mercury*, and the *Nation*.

Yolande Du Bois, the only child of W. E. B. Du Bois, was considered one of the most eligible women of the Talented Tenth. Though she may have loved another man, her status and family did not give her the freedom to make her own choice about marriage.

That summer, Cullen took a job as a waiter in Atlantic City, not far from his family's summer home in Pleasantville. He wrote several poems based on that experience.

If counting the Du Bois family and Witter Bynner as friends wasn't enough, Cullen soon found others seeking him out. At the NAACP annual ball, writer James Weldon Johnson wanted to help up-and-coming black talent. He planned to introduce a few talented artists to Carl Van Vechten, the famed writer and photographer. He chose Countee Cullen and Langston Hughes. Van Vechten was impressed and offered to help both poets by publishing their work, but Cullen declined the offer. He was determined to find success on his own.

More connections soon followed. Cullen attended the Opportunity Dinners held by the Urban League and their magazine, *Opportunity*. There, he met Frederick Lewis Allen, a literary scout for Harper & Brothers.

By his senior year, 1925, Cullen saw major movement in his poetic and academic life. He was elected to Phi Beta Kappa, the oldest academic honor society in the country. He won first prize in the Witter Bynner Poetry Contest as well as *Poetry* magazine's John Reed Memorial Prize for the poem "Threnody for a Brown Girl," and *Crisis's* Amy Spingarn Award for "Two Moods of Love." He also came in second place for *Palm's* poetry contest with "Wisdom Cometh with the Years" and in *Opportunity's* first poetry contest with "To One Who Said Me Nay." In addition to these contests, Cullen's poetry was included in Alain Locke's groundbreaking anthology, *The New Negro*. With all this success, it is no wonder that he capped it off by being accepted into Harvard University's master's program.

COLOR (1925) AND HARVARD

Ending his undergraduate years as a Phi Beta Kappa inductee was a remarkable achievement. However, an even bigger accomplishment was reached when Harper & Brothers offered to publish Cullen's first book.

Color was published in 1925. Cullen was only twenty-two years old. He dedicated the work to his foster parents. It contained seventy-four poems divided up into four parts, and it received favorable reviews.

With his first book published and a number of poetry awards under his belt, Cullen entered Harvard's master's program. He had the great fortune to attend a class with Robert Silliman Hillyer. Hillyer had become an instructor at Harvard only two years after graduating from the university himself. He was also the president of the New England Poetry Club. In addition, he was a Phi Beta Kappa scholar from Tufts University and had studied at the University of Copenhagen. Eager to impress, Cullen was shocked to find his first assignment returned with a D grade. Hillyer believed in Cullen's talent but thought his writing needed refinement. The two worked closely together, eventually forming a deep friendship.

With the excitement around *Color*, Cullen was offered many speaking opportunities and was interviewed by several newspapers and magazines. He headlined events alongside great artists like James Weldon Johnson, J. Rosamond Johnson, and musician Taylor Gordon.

While the success and awards gave him more access outside of Harlem, Cullen still faced discrimination. In the spring of 1926, a month before he was to graduate from Harvard, the Civic Club invited him to speak at the Emerson Hotel in Baltimore. When he arrived at Baltimore's train station, Civic Club officials met him. The hotel management had learned that the featured speaker was black, but it was against the hotel's policy to allow black guests. The Civic Club sent him a letter telling him that he wouldn't be allowed to speak, but they had just missed him. Cullen, angered and humiliated, had boarded the next train back to Boston.

He threw himself into his final examinations and thought of getting a job. He also felt pressure to write another book. Meanwhile, he continued to publish his poetry, winning second prize in a *Crisis* contest for the poem "Thoughts in a Zoo."

THE WORLD AT HOME AND ABROAD

That summer, the church honored Reverend Cullen for his years of service with an all-expense-paid trip to Jerusalem for him and his family. They would also make stops in various European cities. Cullen soaked in the experience. He was enamored by the ship and took every opportunity to explore every port where they stopped. In Paris, he was taken with the sights. He was eager to try speaking French, which he had studied for years. From there, the Cullens took a train to Marseilles and boarded another ship to cross the Mediterranean Sea. They stopped in Alexandria, Beirut, and Haifa. Finally they made it to Jerusalem. The reverend was in awe of the holy sites: the Church of the Holy Sepulchre, the Church of Simon the Cyrenian, the ascension stone.

From Jerusalem, they traveled to Cairo and saw the Pyramids at Giza and the Sphinx. They rode the Nile up to the Red Sea. They returned to Europe, stopping in Rome, where they stood in front of the graves of poets Shelley and Keats. From Italy, they went on to Switzerland. The trip inspired many new poems. After a summer of adventure, Countee Cullen returned to the United States, ready to begin a new chapter of his life.

Leaving academia for the first time, Cullen took a job as an assistant editor for *Opportunity*. His talents impressed Charles Spurgeon Johnson, the magazine's editor. With the position came another prospect: a column. Cullen used his column, "The Dark Tower," to write reviews of books and Broadway shows. He also used it as an opportunity to introduce new writers to the public. By this point, he was friends with many artists, and he enjoyed being able to help promote them.

Countee and Reverend Cullen ride camels around the pyramids of Giza during a stop on their first trip abroad.

Cullen attended parties and events thrown by various socialites. There, he met with old friends and made new contacts. That December, he won a $500 prize in literature from the Harmon Foundation for *Color*. The success brought many new opportunities Cullen's way.

By now, great thinkers like Du Bois were championing the **New Negro movement**. It was quickly becoming a reality, and nowhere more so than in Harlem. Black artists, thinkers, philanthropists, and socialites were gathering together to create vast networks of opportunities for themselves. They called it the Harlem Renaissance.

Cullen was one of the leading voices in this emerging group. With him were other writers, such as Arna Bontemps, Jean Toomer, Claude McKay, Langston Hughes, Walter White, Rudolph Fisher, Jessie Redmon Fauset, and Zora Neale Hurston. In addition to writing, talent was flourishing in music, visual art, theater, and dance.

The Cotton Club was a hot spot of the Harlem Renaissance. This gangster-owned, whites-only club featured iconic black jazz artists such as Cab Calloway, Duke Ellington, and others.

Cullen continued to publish in magazines, such as *Harper's*, *Poetry*, *Fire*, *Palms*, *Crisis*, and others, but he was also eager to publish another book. From his newly published poems and other new writing, he was sure he could produce a book to surpass, if not match, *Color*. His friends, however, discouraged the idea. They didn't think it was a good idea to publish again so soon after his first book.

DRAWING LINES: CULLEN AND HUGHES ON RACE AND AESTHETIC (1927)

In 1927, Cullen's second book, *Copper Sun*, was published by Harper & Brothers. Divided into five sections and containing fifty-eight poems, the book was held in stark contrast to *Color*. There were more poems about love than about race in this book. The first section, entitled "Color," contained just seven poems, but it held one of Cullen's most famous poems, "From the Dark Tower." Dedicated to Charles S. Johnson, the poem affirmed a better future for black people. Another famous poem, "One Day We Played a Game" was a love poem dedicated to Yolande Du Bois. The section entitled "Varia" held poems Cullen wrote while on his trip abroad with Reverend Cullen. It included "At the Wailing Wall in Jerusalem" and "Cor Cordium" written at the Shelley Memorial.

Despite the gems within, his second collection received mixed reviews. The book was seen as sophomoric and garnered little acclaim. Critics said the book did not live up to the expectations set by *Color*. It was Cullen's first taste of disappointment. Fortunately, there were distractions available.

Despite some criticism of his recent work, Cullen was invited to many social gatherings. He met lifelong friends, colleagues, and new artists. Though he was determined to make it on his own, Cullen's youth and talent drew special notice. He built friendships

THE ROARING TWENTIES AND THE NEW NEGRO

The end of World War I ushered in a time of great prosperity. The 1920s were all glitz and glamor for the upper class. Saloons were fueled by the need for bootleg alcohol due to Prohibition. The exuberance of the time earned the decade its nickname, the Roaring Twenties. Gatherings varied from opulent, crowded parties to more conservative, intellectual ones. The fervor for such activities—and access to alcohol—gave prominence to gangs. Jazz music and hotspots like the Cotton Club—run by gangster Owen Madden—attracted white people to Harlem.

For middle- and upper-class blacks, these social events fostered networking opportunities. Miss A'Lelia Walker, a black heiress with a love of the arts, held the most extravagant parties. She owned a house on 136th Street, which she heavily decorated. With a gold-painted piano and artwork covering the walls, her home helped her connect aspiring artists with established agents and producers. In the main room, large prints of two poems hung: "The Weary Blues," by Langston Hughes, and "From the Dark Tower," by Countee Cullen. The room became known as "The Dark Tower."

not only with other up-and-comers like Langston Hughes and Arna Bontemps, but with more established artists like writer and photographer Alain Locke.

As his social life grew, Cullen used his new connections for professional growth. When he was asked to edit *Caroling Dusk*, an anthology of work by black writers, Cullen tapped into his network of friends. He knew their work and wanted to amass as much quality work as he could. Each contributor wrote his or her own biographical statement. These statements showcased the variety of voices and thoughts among the black artists.

In his own statement, Cullen gave a glimpse into his life and how he saw himself. He described his upbringing in a conservative, religious atmosphere. He wrote that his principle concern in life was to make peace between his pagan desires and his Christian beliefs. But he believed he could solve the problem in his lifetime. Cullen was also extremely opposed to all racial segregation. The most interesting thing about the statement was his thoughts on his education. Cullen had been educated in New York public schools, New York University, and Harvard University, but he regretted never having attended what he called a racial school. In part, he was referring to his own privilege. He was also confronting the idea of racial uplift. Many of his contemporaries believed that blacks should only write and portray the best aspects of their race. This idea was widely promoted by people like W. E. B. Du Bois and Langston Hughes. It meant that black characters had to be superhuman, but Cullen wanted to write what he saw as the truth. He wanted to include the good and bad.

His regrets drew from a number of sources. Cullen had always been fascinated with his racial heritage and identity. His education, however, had been at a white institution, and his influences were mostly European.

A year earlier, in 1926, Langston Hughes—who would be viewed as Cullen's **antithesis**—wrote a scathing essay. "The Negro Artists and the Racial Mountain" accused an unnamed poet of

Carl Van Vechten shot this portrait of Langston Hughes in 1936.

wanting to write like a white poet. By writing like white poets, Hughes believed, this poet wanted to be white himself. Hughes did not want this poet to be considered a Negro poet. The essay was a thinly veiled insult to Cullen. In his biographical statement, Cullen was thus directly responding to Hughes's accusation.

Cullen's admission that he wished he had attended a racial school is even more interesting when considering his job as the editor of the anthology. Despite his regrets, he does not limit his collection to poets of a more racial school. Cullen valued and wanted to emphasize the diversity of black writers. He called the anthology one of "Verse by Negro poets" as opposed to "Negro Verse." The anthology, *Caroling Dusk*, was published in 1927.

An illustrated version of his ballad was also published as *The Ballad of the Brown Girl*. The images, drawn by Charles Cullen (no relation), depicted the events of the poem as they unfolded. It included a dramatic two-page spread for the murder-suicide scene. Charles Cullen had previously illustrated Cullen's first book, *Color*.

YOLANDE DU BOIS AND COUNTEE CULLEN

The year 1927 was pivotal for Cullen in his personal life as well. He asked Yolande Du Bois for her hand in marriage.

Since their courtship when Cullen was attending NYU, the couple had been exchanging letters. They became very close, but Cullen was not always ready to meet Yolande's needs. She chastised him for not responding to her letters. Yolande wanted more frequent correspondence. Instead, Cullen spent more energy on his correspondence with his high school friend, intellectual and teacher Harold Jackman. Their deep correspondence, especially when compared to his exchanges with Yolande, has caused some researchers to wonder about Cullen's sexuality.

The engagement would be a long one. The two had never been dating exclusively, but they were both jealous of each

Carl Van Vechten was enamored with black artists, documenting the Harlem Renaissance in his photography, especially at Harlemite gatherings.

Countee Cullen

other's relationships. Yolande was rumored to have been seeing jazzman Jimmie Lunceford for years. Cullen wrote to and flirted with other women as well. Because they lived in separate cities, it was difficult to maintain their relationship. For its duration, Du Bois stayed in Baltimore and Cullen in Harlem. The yearlong engagement would not help them resolve their issues.

In addition to their personal problems, the couple's parents interfered with their relationship. From the beginning, W. E. B. Du Bois had been fond of Cullen. He thought Cullen would be a good match for his daughter, and he had no problems letting Yolande know his feelings.

That his only daughter was to marry such an accomplished man delighted Du Bois. It was a match not just worthy of her, but by extension, of him. Rumors that Yolande had her heart set on another did not deter this feeling. To many, this marriage would be the crown jewel of the Harlem Renaissance.

A DECLINE IN THE YEARS AHEAD

As 1927 drew to a close, Cullen had reached a high point in his career. In the span of six years, he had become one of the prominent forces of the Harlem Renaissance. Publishing his first book in 1925 and three more in 1927, Cullen's star seemed on the rise. His work had drawn immediate notice and praise from influential people in the arts community.

Color was still held in high esteem, though his other books were not as favorably reviewed. He published poems in magazines and frequently placed in competitions. He gave readings, held a prominent position at a magazine, and did interviews with newspapers and magazines. The early years of his career would be regarded as his most productive. They also marked the moment he became a symbol of the new black image, christened by his engagement and marriage into a prominent family.

CHAPTER THREE

SELF-CRITICISM

The wedding of Yolande Du Bois and Countee Cullen was Harlem's social event of the year. W. E. B. Du Bois was heavily involved in the planning. He had a say in everything, from the number of guests to the bride's dress. To many, the wedding was not just about the union of two young people. Harlem's middle class saw it as a symbolic christening of the New Negro. The pageantry had to match, if not surpass, expectations.

In April 1928, the two exchanged vows. The ceremony was held at the Salem Methodist Church and officiated by Reverend Cullen. Langston Hughes and Arna Bontemps were ushers. Harold Jackman was the best man. Yolande had sixteen bridesmaids. According to one biographer, a choir of songbirds accompanied the bride down the aisle in true decadent fashion.

The reception was held in the Dark Tower at A'Lelia Walker's home. People gathered outside to catch a glimpse of the action. Prominent artists in literature, scholarship, music, visual art, and dance were schmoozing and having a good time. All those in

Opposite: Yolande Du Bois's dress and her maids were hot items for gossip and speculation in the days leading up to her wedding.

attendance were treated to a glamorous social event. The newlyweds were treated like royalty. Two branches of the Talented Tenth had been joined. Many hoped that this union would usher in an era free from the shackles of negative stereotypes.

But problems in the marriage quickly surfaced. After the wedding and a brief honeymoon in Philadelphia, Yolande returned to teaching in Baltimore. Cullen left with Jackman and his father to start his Guggenheim Fellowship in Paris, France. The distance between the couple made the relationship difficult, and deep interference from their parents made things even worse. Reverend Cullen and Yolande did not get along well. W. E. B. Du Bois frequently advised Yolande on her marriage. He encouraged her to support her husband's career and writing. But both Yolande and Cullen were busy with their own responsibilities. They had truly separate lives.

THE GUGGENHEIM YEARS AND *THE BLACK CHRIST AND OTHER POEMS* (1929)

Cullen's Guggenheim Fellowship allowed him to focus solely on his art. While his job at *Opportunity* was rewarding, aside from his column, he had seen very little of his own publication. He left his post at *Opportunity*, excited for the chance of a lifetime.

Cullen was the second black American to earn a fellowship. He was appointed as a 1928 fellow. For twelve months, he would write a group of narrative poems and the libretto for an opera. He chose to spend the year in France.

In Paris, Cullen spent his time in the company of other Americans. He developed close relationships with artists such as Augusta Savage and Palmer Hayden. The artists formed a group to support and motivate each other in their endeavors. That summer, Reverend Cullen visited his son during what had become a yearly European vacation. Yolande visited as well, but even then, the marriage did not improve.

Cullen spent much of his time as a Guggenheim Fellow taking in sites such as the Arc de Triomphe and the Eiffel Tower.

THE GREAT DEPRESSION

The stock market crash of 1929 signified the end of the Roaring Twenties. With it, some have argued, the Harlem Renaissance also came to a close. Wall Street lost more than $30 billion in the New York Stock Exchange. This financial loss contributed to the Great Depression. When World War I ended, stockbrokers anticipated continuous, permanent economic growth. They took many high-stakes risks and there was a lot of speculation happening in the markets. There were few laws to guide business practices. Many politicians believed that a free market would guide business practices without government involvement. For years, the courts had struck down laws regulating business during what would be called the Lochner Era.

As the Great Depression took hold, unemployment levels skyrocketed. Factories, banks, businesses, and farms went bankrupt. Soup kitchens and churches had scores of people lined up for help. In the winters, people covered themselves in newspapers to stay warm. Suicide rates increased out of desperation and the lack of available help. President Herbert Hoover failed to adequately address the situation. He believed the economic downturn would be temporary. Because he believed in small government, he was reluctant to let the federal government intervene. Instead, he appealed to states and the private sector to come to people's aid. When he finally started to intervene, it was largely to help businesses, not the struggling American people. Hoover's actions were too little too late. His failures led the way for Franklin D. Roosevelt to win the election in 1932 and implement his New Deal policies, creating new jobs and opportunities for Americans.

Cullen wrote many poems about his life in Paris, but his best-known work from that time was not related to his Paris adventures. The poem was titled "The Black Christ." It would become the title poem for his next book, published in 1929. *The Black Christ and Other Poems* was not well regarded, even among his most ardent supporters. Critics began to question Cullen's productivity and lamented that his work had not matured as they had hoped.

Major change began to happen in Harlem in 1929. The Great Depression brought hardship to all. However, already marginalized black people in particular faced even greater problems. The extravagant parties, hot clubs, and roaring lifestyles of the 1920s rapidly dissipated. Increased rent, unemployment, and racism would lead to a series of riots.

DIVORCE AND CULLEN'S SEXUALITY

Cullen was away for the first year of the Great Depression, extending his time as a Guggenheim Fellow. With so much time apart, his marriage to Yolande suffered. Trouble was evident as early as six months into their marriage. W. E. B. Du Bois even tried to advise Cullen about the relationship. He thought that Yolande was being timid in consummating the marriage. Despite Du Bois's involvement, however, the marriage seemed doomed.

Cullen's travels seemed like an excuse to escape his wife's presence. Yolande visited her mother in Paris and tried to reconcile with Cullen. They sent letters back and forth, but after a while the only solution seemed to be divorce. Yolande wrote that while she wanted to reunite, it was up to Cullen. Ultimately, the marriage would end. In April 1929, she filed for divorce.

There were always problems with the marriage, but Yolande's main reason for the divorce was Cullen's sexuality. Cullen admitted to his wife that he was gay. She wrote to her father about Cullen

W. E. B. Du Bois's enthusiasm for Cullen's work seemed to have more to do with the image of the Talented Tenth than the blossoming artist himself.

on May 23, 1929. She told him that she had heard the rumors that Cullen was gay but did not believe them until he came out to her.

Biographers do not all agree on Cullen's sexuality. Aside from Yolande's letter to her father, there is no definitive proof that Cullen was gay. Adding to researchers' confusion is the fact that Cullen later married another woman.

Biographers speculate that many of the Harlem Renaissance men were gay. Langston Hughes, Alain Locke, and Harold Jackman all had close relationships with men. But with homophobic attitudes, it is unlikely any of them were publicly open about their sexuality. Their secrecy thus makes it difficult to know for sure. Dates, rendezvous, and relationships were kept private. People gossiped about the artists they suspected were gay, but this gossip does not amount to fact. Sharing their secret lives was, in part, what drew these men close as a group of friends.

Critics have guessed that Cullen's work, like Hughes's, is coded with gay symbolism. The contrast between Christian values and pagan needs in his poetry is sometimes used to explain Cullen's sexuality. In addition, his upbringing by Reverend Cullen is also cited as explanation for his secrecy about his sexuality.

When the marriage ended, Yolande returned to the United States. Cullen kept up a good relationship with the elder Du Bois, who still had high hopes for the poet. It's unclear whether Cullen knew Yolande confessed his sexuality to her father. In the fall of 1930, he returned to Harlem, ending his extended stay in France.

ONE WAY TO HEAVEN (1932) AND FREDERICK DOUGLASS JUNIOR HIGH SCHOOL

Struggling to write more poetry, Cullen threw himself into his next book. He was now focused on a novel. One Way to Heaven was published in 1932. It received little attention from critics and readers. That same year, Carolyn Cullen, the woman who had opened him to art and beauty, passed away on October 5.

Cullen was reluctant to give up writing full time, but the hardships of the Great Depression meant he needed steady work. He decided to look for teaching jobs. Early in his career, teaching was not what Cullen had wanted to do with his life. He had always valued education, however, and knew the responsibility a teacher held. During his undergraduate years at NYU, he had taken four educational courses. These included the history of education, educational psychology, elements in methods of teaching high school English, and principles and problems of education. Cullen believed he had the skills and knowledge to be an effective teacher. He needed the work, but he also worried that teaching would interfere with his writing.

In 1934, Cullen was offered a position at Frederick Douglass Junior High in New York City. He taught English and French. He wanted to give enthusiastic students the chance to take creative writing classes. He pushed the administration to allow him to teach these classes. He hosted competitions for his class and even secured publication for a few talented students. One of his students was James Baldwin. Baldwin would become a famous writer in his own right. He followed in Cullen's footsteps and went to DeWitt Clinton High School. He even joined the *Magpie* as the literary editor. Baldwin took the opportunity to publish an interview with Cullen for the magazine.

Cullen was a highly successful teacher. However, he used some unorthodox methods. He took his class outside, taught memorization techniques, and emphasized his students' unlimited potential. Ultimately he became more teacher than poet. Less and less of his work appeared in magazines, and he had not published another book. Focusing on teaching, his reputation as a Harlem Renaissance poet began to decline.

HARLEM IN THE 1930s

Cullen kept busy in other ways besides teaching. He also became involved in politics, especially those concerning black people in Harlem. The Great Depression had hit the neighborhood hard. Life became even more difficult, however, due to government policies targeting blacks. The National Housing Act of 1934 was supposed to make mortgages more affordable. Instead, it classified neighborhoods with poor minorities as high risk. People in Harlem were denied mortgages and other financial services. They were forced into poorer neighborhoods. The poor got poorer. Those without cars or bus fare were deprived of their freedom of movement. They were stuck in Harlem, which quickly became a ghetto.

For about a year after the policy took effect, protesters picketed in front of white businesses. They organized boycotts of stores that wouldn't hire blacks. People living in Harlem were angry about the prejudice they continued to face. On March 19, 1935, a young black boy was caught shoplifting and taken in by police. He was ultimately let go, but rumors about what had happened to him spread quickly. People believed that the boy had been injured, or even murdered. An ambulance at the scene incensed the growing crowd and added the appearance of truth to the rumor. The angered black population had had enough. A riot erupted. People began hurling rocks and what objects they had. They caused a considerable amount damage.

With many people demanding improvements, the city was quick to react. A committee was formed to investigate issues in Harlem. Cullen joined the board of the subcommittee on education. The committee found that no elementary school had been built in Harlem since 1925. By 1934, Harlem's population had greatly increased. More space was needed for all these students. The commission's report also condemned police brutality and the

In 1964, Harlem would riot again for much of the same reasons the 1935 committee had cited: no jobs, no rights, and insecurity.

lack of economic opportunity and social reform. The insecurity created by these kinds of discrimination, they believed, was the root causes of the 1935 riot.

The committee concluded that without significant changes, future riots would ensue. In particular, the subcommittee proposed building a new playground. They also hoped to air a radio program featuring First Lady Eleanor Roosevelt. However, the situation did not change significantly. Riots would emerge out of Harlem sporadically for decades to follow.

THE MEDEA AND SOME POEMS (1935) AND ENGAGING THE THEATER

In 1935 Cullen finally published another book, *The Medea and Some Poems*. The book featured his translation of *Medea*, the ancient Greek tragedy by Euripides, and twenty-seven new poems. The translation was the first major ancient Greek translation by a black person in the twentieth century.

Cullen imagined his version of *Medea* on the stage. He envisioned actress Rose McClendon as the main character. Unfortunately, McClendon passed away the following year, in 1936, at the age of fifty-two. She would not perform the role, though Carl Van Vechten had photographed her in a Medea costume. Instead, in 1940, Cullen's *Medea* opened at Atlanta University with Dorothy Ateca as the lead.

By the time *Medea* opened, Cullen had set his sights on the theater. He cowrote a script with Owen Dodson entitled *They Seek a City*. The play bore witness to the Great Migration and industrialization of America. It followed the story of a black farmer and his family as they moved from the cotton-picking South to the factory-line North. However, the script was never put into production.

In this 1940 publicity shot by Carl Van Vechten, the actress Dorothy Ateca is dressed regally as the titular character of Cullen's *Medea*.

Eager to find new opportunities, Cullen searched the country for a teaching position at a university. Many of the Harlem Renaissance's writers had moved out of Harlem. Some were teaching at universities. Cullen wanted a similar prestigious teaching position. Unfortunately, no job was forthcoming. Many colleges and universities faced financial issues at this time. They were not looking to take on new staff.

Finally, Cullen was offered a position in New Orleans. He was eager to accept the position, but Reverend Cullen had become ill. Cullen had to decline the position to take care of his ailing father. In 1937, he began courting Ida Mae Roberson, whom he had known for some time. At the time they began seeing each other, Roberson was seeking a divorce from her first husband.

Professionally, Cullen returned to the prospect of the theater. He adapted his novel into a three-act play entitled *Heaven's My Home*. It was only ever staged for one performance, and it got mediocre reviews. Cullen and Claude McKay thought that they might work on a project together. They attempted various projects, but to no avail. By this point, Cullen was starting to grow ill, often having stomach problems.

Meanwhile, Europe was in upheaval. European countries had suffered through the Great Depression just as badly as America. New governments rose up. On September 1, 1939, Nazi Germany invaded Poland, thus beginning World War II.

THE LOST ZOO (1940), MY LIVES AND HOW I LOST THEM (1942), AND MARRIAGE TO IDA

Cullen had the idea to work in a new medium: children's books. His first children's book, *The Lost Zoo*, was published in 1940. The book, "cowritten" with his cat Christopher, tells the stories of the animals who did not make it onto Noah's Ark. The book contained moral messages for children about kindness and acceptance. It garnered success, as children were enamored with the idea of a talking cat.

That same year, Ida and Cullen were married. They lived in an apartment for a time before finding a home north of New York City. They took Revered Cullen with them due to his health. Cullen's own health was also deteriorating, but he kept working.

His next published work was another children's book. *My Lives and How I Lost Them* details the various lives of Christopher Cat with help from Countee Cullen. This book did not go over well. It did not have the same whimsical nature that people loved from *The Lost Zoo*.

ST. LOUIS WOMAN (1946)

Meanwhile, Cullen was still working on breaking into theater. Since the 1930s, he had been working tirelessly on adapting Arna Bontemps's novel, *God Sends Sunday*. He imagined it as a Broadway musical entitled *St. Louis Woman*. The endeavor had started in 1930, but it now gained momentum with help from Bontemps and Langston Hughes.

While the play was being produced for Broadway, controversy erupted. Actress Lena Horne was slated to play the title character; however, she turned the role down when she was advised against its seedy subject matter. The story revolved around prostitutes and pimps. It was considered an insult to the New Negro movement. A great deal of work had been done to promote a higher-class image of blacks. Showing them as pimps and prostitutes on stage went against the New Negro movement's aims. Cullen was enraged. He was especially incensed when he learned that many critics had not even read the script before denouncing the play.

Cullen invited critics to a dramatic reading of the play. He brought sketches and ideas from the show's plans. Despite his best efforts, most critics refused to acknowledge the work on its own merit. Instead, they supported the idea of racial uplift, which Cullen had been battling his whole life. He did not want to be limited by showing black characters in only positive roles. He wanted the freedom to show their lives in a multitude of ways. It was more honest, he believed, to show black characters as real humans with all their complexities.

The musical was scheduled to open in the fall of 1945, but it was postponed. In the meantime, he and Owen Dodson cowrote *The Third Fourth of July*. This one-act play was published in 1946. The play followed the story of a black family and a white family who lived next door to one another. The families do not get along. Throughout the play, the white family uses racial slurs and insults. Things change when a telegram is misdelivered to the white family. They get the news that their neighbor's son has died in the war. In the end, the white mother delivers the message to the black mother and they share in their grief. The play was not staged in Cullen's lifetime.

DEATH

Cullen's health issues had taken their toll. He suffered from severe headaches, high blood pressure, and stomach problems. In addition, the stress he put on himself to produce work and the controversy surrounding it contributed to his declining health. Eventually, his kidney failed. On January 9, 1946, Cullen suffered a cerebral hemorrhage. He passed away at age forty-three.

Under heavy rain, three thousand people attended his funeral. Longtime friends, supporters, and others paid their respects at the Salem Methodist Episcopal Church. His students from Frederick Douglass also attended.

The funeral was a modest affair. A few of Cullen's poems were read, as well as a telegram sent by writer Clifford Odets. Mourners said their farewells to an open casket. Cullen's friends

Arna Bontemps, Harold Jackman, Langston Hughes, and Owen Dodson served as pallbearers.

Writing for *Crisis*, W. E. B. Du Bois put down a woeful obituary. Du Bois had great respect for the poet he had once seen as the paragon of the New Negro. He understood that Cullen's life was full of potential but ultimately became incomplete.

Before his death, Cullen had been working on a collection of his best poetry. *On These I Stand* was posthumously published one year after his death. It included only six new poems. *St. Louis Woman* would open on Broadway for 113 shows in March. Years ago, Carolyn Cullen had taught him to make music with the piano and his words. The play was Cullen's final encore.

THE DIMMED STAR

Cullen's life was relatively short. His career had spanned just over twenty years. In that time, he published extensively. He wrote four books of poetry, a novel, two children's books, and a number of plays. He also edited an anthology. Cullen's name and interviews were in newspapers all over the country. He traveled the world and gained an incredible amount of popularity for himself and black art in general.

Still, Cullen's relationship with race would cloud his legacy for decades after his death. His name would fade under the bright light of other Harlem Renaissance artists, such as Langston Hughes. Only a small portion of Cullen's poems would be anthologized in decades to come.

Cullen's papers now reside in the Amistad Research Center at Tulane University and the Countee Cullen-Harold Jackman Memorial Collection of Atlanta University. New scholarship on the Harlem Renaissance and Cullen's work has helped bring his name back into prominence. Historians analyze his work and try to explain how a star that once shone so brightly with artistic talent faded so quickly.

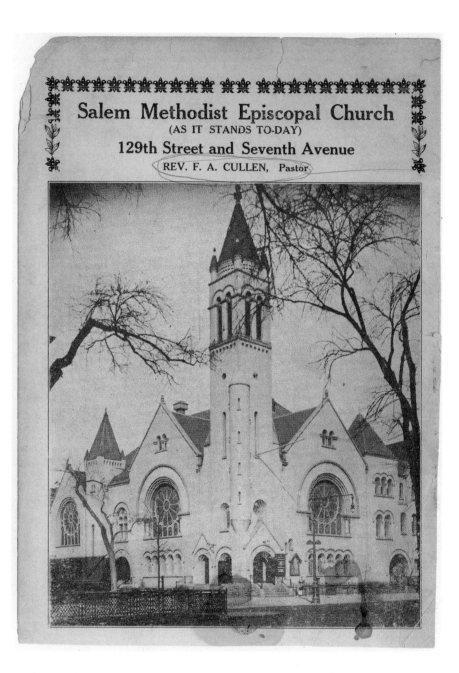

Salem Methodist Episcopal Church
(AS IT STANDS TO-DAY)
129th Street and Seventh Avenue
REV. F. A. CULLEN, Pastor

Cullen's funeral was held at Salem Methodist Episcopal Church, where his father had long served as pastor.

The Work of Countee Cullen

"A thing of beauty is a joy for ever:
Its loveliness increases; it will never
Pass into nothingness; but still will keep
A bower quiet for us, and a sleep
Full of sweet dreams, and health, and
    quiet breathing."

—John Keats, *Endymion: Book I*

CHAPTER FOUR

TO YOU WHO READ MY BOOK

Though Countee Cullen ended his career writing mostly prose, his poetry takes center stage. By investigating his poetry, modern readers gain insight into Cullen's sensibilities, beliefs, and techniques of writing. Examining Cullen's verse shows readers how his poems often conflict with statements he made in interviews.

THEMES

Cullen's work orbits similar universal themes. He dealt with these ideas in varying degrees of nuance. Among his popular themes were race and racism, life and death, sex and sexuality, and beauty as the main purpose of art. He also explored love—romantic, familial, and of the self. Religion was a common theme as well, as he explored paganism versus Christianity. These themes were often related. For example, love, race, and beauty would unite in his poems as love of race and accepting the beauty of race. These three themes would come together often in Cullen's work.

Opposite: Cullen's children's books were a success due to the fascination readers had with his coauthor, Christopher, an intelligent and communicative cat.

An example of themes converging can be found in the poem "A Brown Girl Dead" from *Color*. The poem is simple enough on the surface. A black girl has died, and this is a portrait of her funeral. Her mother sold a wedding ring to buy a white dress for the girl to be buried in. The speaker then exclaims that if the girl were able to see herself, she'd be so happy that she would "dance and sing" at her own funeral.

Cullen only needs two **stanzas** to leave a complex and layered image. Key parts elevate the poem. For one, the speaker affirms the girl's beauty, likening her to the Virgin Mary. The poem emphasizes that she is covered in white, from the flowers on her breast to the candles at her feet.

It is the last line of the first stanza that starts to complicate the poem. Lord Death admires her. Giving Death this title not only emphasizes death's power, but it also suggests the **archaic** term for husband. The brown girl is not only an image of the Christian Madonna but also of the pagan Persephone. In Greek literature, Persephone marries Hades, lord of the dead. The white dress becomes not a burial shroud, but a wedding dress. The wedding ring that was sold could be the girl's or the mother's (the pronouns can be read either way). In the end, the funeral is transformed into a wedding celebration. The girl, if she were alive, would celebrate.

The poem is in the "Color" section of *Color*. It is tempting then, to read the poem with an emphasis on race. The white candles, flowers, and dress could be read as symbols of white prejudice against the dead body of a black girl. But the poem's ending, in which the girl celebrates how she looks in white, does not make sense in that interpretation. This is not to say that the poem isn't about race. It certainly contains some racial elements. At this time, black women were often compared to white women and deemed inferior. Cullen showed this dead girl as so beautiful and desirable that Death takes her to wife like a Greek goddess of old. In Cullen's strongest poetry, he creates layered images like this one.

The views were not always consistent. In one poem, paganism would be considered virtuous—especially in terms of the gifts from having African ancestry—but in another poem, Cullen would show Christianity as a path of redemption for black people. As any poet, Cullen reserved the right to contradict himself. Some truths, however, could not be so easily turned over.

A constant theme throughout his body of work was the issue of racism. He wrote emphatically not just about individual racial prejudice but about the systemic forces of racism in society. Both individual and institutional experiences of racism were deeply moving. Cullen and other writers explored the topic with great sophistication. In Cullen's work, as in others', racism is always rejected. There were no qualifiers. Racism was always wrong.

In effect, Cullen's poems started on the side of hope. But over the years, his poetry showed an amount of resignation. His most famous poem in regards to racism is "Incident." The speaker of the poem is a man looking back at when he visited Baltimore when he was eight years old. While going about the city, he sees a white boy around his age and smiles at him. The boy responds by yelling a racial slur. Though he would stay in Baltimore for eight months, that's all that the speaker would remember from his stay.

The poem uses a singsong quality. Its childlike musicality stands in contrast to the serious situation. The effect of the discrimination was so great that the child, now grown, could not remember anything else about his time in the city. His past had impacted the present-day adult. This poem is a prime example of how Cullen's form aided the function of the poem.

For Cullen, race was a double-edged sword. While he unabashedly rejected racism, he—like many artists of the time—reaffirmed racial stereotypes. One of these stereotypes, which persist today, is of the "noble savage." In literature, a noble savage is an idealized character who embodies the outsider who has not been corrupted by civilization. In "Atlantic City Waiter," Cullen describes a black waiter. The waiter is able to move gracefully

Marcus Garvey promoted the idea that blacks should embrace their African heritage and even return to Africa and establish an all-black nation there. The images he ignited with his pan-African ideas gripped young artists like Cullen.

among the diners, and this is said to be due to his African heritage and his people's gift for rhythm and dance. In this view, paganism is not just a strange and exotic lifestyle but also a direct inheritance from Africa. One of the justifications for enslaving Africans was that they were savage, or pagan, and needed to be civilized.

Part of the civilizing process was conversion to Christianity. Adopting this new religion was a means to quash the inferiorities that Christians believed that black people possessed. Blacks were associated with Africa, paganism, savagery, passion, and strong physical ability. Whites, on the other hand, were associated with Europe, Christianity, civilization, intellect and art. Cullen's poetry dealing with Africa upheld this contradiction. Curiously, the sentiments in his poems did not match the viewpoints on art and race that he gave in interviews. He was certainly not inclined (as a poet himself) to believe art was only the invention of white people.

Christianity versus paganism could also be interpreted as another struggle for the poet. The religious struggle may have symbolized a different, personal battle. Cullen may have been writing to express the pressure he felt to conform to a homophobic, heterosexual society. For instance, the poem "Tableau" follows a black boy and a white boy walking arm-in-arm in public. Both black people and white people disapprove. The boys, however, ignore them and continue on their walk undeterred. The poem can be read purely in terms of race. The boys break all decency and mix the races in a segregated society. Being arm-in-arm could symbolize a brotherhood, as in "brothers in arms." Could this poem simply pair with "Incident," which appears only three pages later? Both poems deal with childhood views of racism.

But if "Tableau" is about racism, why would the black people in the poem disapprove of the boys' friendship? After all, Cullen attended a majority white school. In addition, the Harlem Renaissance had a large white audience. It was supported by white patrons and relied on white publishers. Black people—and some white people—were already finding avenues of desegregation. Some were adamant to challenge the legality of segregation policies.

A different reading could shed more light on the poem's intention. Perhaps the people in the poem were not scandalized by the boys' races, but by the affection they shared. The imagery of thunder and lightning in the poem could describe the friction, or heat, between the boys.

Perhaps Cullen's biggest theme—though not his most popular one—was beauty. Cullen believed that a poet's job was to create art that was beautiful to behold. This would become the definitive assessment of his work. His detractors say his poems are simplistic, metrically repetitive, or pointless, but they cannot say they are not beautiful.

In "To John Keats, Poet. At Spring Time," the speaker cannot contain his delight at the beauty of spring. Beauty is the chief reason for the poem. It is addressed to John Keats, who felt beauty very deeply. Cullen's ability to create beauty indicates strength in his poetry.

Beauty is a concept that is entrenched in social and cultural attitudes. Centuries of discrimination led many blacks to believe they were not beautiful, smart, or good. The most famous investigation of this phenomenon was the 1940s "doll test." In this psychological test, children of different races were given the option to play with a white doll or a black doll. The majority of children, black and white, chose to play with the white doll. They even chose the white doll when researchers asked the children which doll looked most like themselves.

Cullen's poems about race often contain affirmations of black beauty. In "To a Brown Boy," he writes that a boy should not mind his reaction to seeing beauty. In this case, the boy sees a beautiful girl with the grace of a queen. So while his critics may consider beauty a superfluous theme, it held importance on many levels.

Cullen, being one of the few Renaissance artists from Harlem, was also one of the last to leave when the Renaissance was over.

COLOR (1925)

Color was by far Cullen's most successful book. It best highlights his poetic skill and it was well received by his peers. As an artistic work and historical document, *Color* laid out the concerns, themes, and obsessions from which Cullen would draw future works. The title section of the book, containing mostly poems on race, drew the most attention.

FORM AND STYLE

One criticism of Cullen's poetry is that neither his style nor his forms ever changed in any significant way. Cullen was most interested in the traditions of the Romantic poets. He was much less interested in the artistic innovations that were happening around him.

Cullen was enamored by the challenge of strict meters and rhymes, though he did, on occasion, manipulate the form to fit the subject matter. His meters were conventional, mostly **iambic**, which was common at the time of metered poetry. Iambic meter is the natural way people speak the English language. Cullen's lines are almost always strictly end rhymed, and he never ventured into **slant rhymes**, or half rhymes. Most of his poems were also broken into stanzas. In shorter poems, the stanzas were individual sentences. In longer poems, they contained two or more sentences.

The poems were heavy with images that elicited ideas rather than emotions. However, his best poetry provided beautiful images, provoking ideas, and searing emotions. His poems were also mostly taken at face value. While Cullen's poems had messages about the world in which he lived, they were not coated in **metaphor** but could often be an **allegory**.

His most quoted poem from that book is "Yet Do I Marvel." The speaker of the poem wonders why, with God being good, there is suffering in the world. From the blind moles in the dirt to the flesh that ages and dies, he wonders at the ugliness around him. Invoking Greek mythological figures such as Sisyphus and Tantalus, the speaker expresses the seeming futility of life. He wants some clue to understand why God would let these things happen. The poem ends on a seemingly different note. The speaker marvels at the fact that God would create a poet that is black and make him sing. Cullen is comparing being a black poet to the punishment of pushing Sisyphus's boulder up a never-ending staircase. It is a futile task that can never be completed.

There seems to be a disconnect between the last two lines and the rest of the poem. To modern audiences, the existence of a black poet could not be the same thing as being doomed to die. This equation is even more haunting coming from a black poet himself. It could be interpreted in many ways. For one, the poem speaks to uneasiness on the part of the poet. His race could be a reason for many to dismiss his poetry.

A more compelling reading of the poem comes from examining the last word: "sing." The associations with this word are tied to the audience's expectations. Singing is often beautiful and emotionally impacting. The poem emphasizes the ugly side of life. Examining the ugly side of American history means invoking slavery, the Civil War, and Jim Crow. It also means having to look closely at daily injustices and discrimination. Faced with all this ugliness, how is it that God could expect a black poet to create beauty? Cullen marvels at the heroic resilience of black people and the wisdom of a God who created this resilience in them.

THE BALLAD OF THE BROWN GIRL (1927)

Cullen's famous poem was taken from an old Kentucky ballad of the same name. However, he made some changes. In the original ballad, a lord goes to his mother for advice on whom to marry. His choices are the lovely fair girl who holds his heart or the rich girl with brown hair. The mother—filled with greed—advises him to marry the rich girl. At the wedding, the fair girl appears and insults the bride. A quarrel follows. Soon all three are dead. The lord's mother has to face the consequences of her ill advice.

In Cullen's poem, a white man named Lord Thomas is encouraged by his mother to leave his white love, Fair London. Instead, he is to marry a wealthy, black woman, the Brown Girl. Fair London attends the wedding and insults the Brown Girl. She says that like should marry like. The white man should not marry what is inferior, a black woman. Lord Thomas refuses to avenge his new wife's honor. Therefore, the Brown Girl kills Fair London, stabbing her with a slim dagger. Lord Thomas grabs the Brown Girl and chokes her to death with her own hair. He then chastises his mother before killing himself. In the end the three lovers are buried together. Fair London and Lord Thomas are put side by side with the Brown Girl lying at their feet.

The original ballad makes an obvious case for valuing love over wealth. But the changes Cullen makes allow for multiple readings, giving the ballad more depth. The poem is often cited as evidence of Cullen's stance on mixed-race affairs. Fair London makes the case at the wedding that like should marry like. She uses the image of a rose: a rose should marry a rose. However, both women are described as beautiful roses in the poem. Fair London is a fresh white rose and the Brown Girl is a dark dying rose. A rose did marry a rose after all, complicating the idea that the poem is only about **miscegenation**, or mixed-race relationships.

The issue of mixed-race relationships is explicit in the poem, but it does not explain Cullen's poor treatment of the Brown Girl. Though Cullen gives the poem racial diversity in its characters, the portrayal of the black woman is a stark contrast to his usual fixation on beauty.

The number of people living in Harlem increased over the years, leaving the streets crowded. When the stock market crashed, Harlem descended into a slum.

Unlike his other poems featuring black women, Cullen's ballad is a stark erasure of them. For instance, both Fair London and Lord Thomas are given names, but the Brown Girl is not. Her death is a gruesome lynching by her own hair. She is buried at the feet of the two white lovers. Despite being desirably rich, her placement at the lovers' feet is a symbol of how low she is compared to them. It may be said that the issue is less about mixed-race relationships and more about race in general. The insult to the Brown Girl is particularly upsetting. She is richer, perhaps as beautiful, and has just married the man Fair London loves. And yet, she can still be insulted with impunity. Worse still is the fact that her new husband will not defend her dignity. Instead, he refuses to defend or avenge her. Despite her advantage and privilege, she is still just a black woman among white people who disdain her for her race.

COPPER SUN (1927)

Cullen's poem "From the Dark Tower," showcases the best *Copper Sun* has to offer. The poem looks forward to the day when blacks themselves, not someone else, will reap the fruits of their own labor. It anticipates a day when black people will be regarded as equals in society and their suffering will end. The last stanza emphasizes the beauty of darkness. The dark night sky is contrasted against the brightest star and describes flowers that cannot bloom in the light. So, while black people must endure pain and wait, something better will come.

Copper Sun was his first book to receive less than stellar reviews. Most of the poems had not matured in form, and the poet had moved away from racial themes. But critics argue that those themes produced some of his best work. The lack of growth is obvious when comparing poems on the same topic from the separate books.

In *Color*, Cullen wrote "To John Keats, Poet. At Spring Time" as an ode to one of his biggest poetic influences. The main concern in the poem is beauty. Keats is admired as a poet who knows beauty best. Addressing Keats, the speaker cannot contain his enthusiasm for this particularly lovely spring. It has enveloped him. Cullen implies a question about the value society places on beauty. He suggests that most people do not hold much value in

Prentiss Taylor's *Christ in Alabama* invokes the harsh realities of slavery: a black man is crucified by King Cotton while a weeping woman looks on.

beauty. The question gives the poem an opening, a level of discovery that one wouldn't expect in a poem about a long-dead poet.

But compare this poem to "To Endymion" in *Copper Sun*. In this poem, Cullen writes about Keats again. This time, however, there is no process of discovery. The poem's title comes from the ancient Greek myth of Endymion. In the story, a handsome shepherd becomes the lover of the moon goddess Selene. Keats rewrote the tale in an epic poem. It makes up four books, published in 1818. In Keats's version, he starts with a praise of beauty, and he follows Endymion on his quest to be united with his love, renamed Cynthia. The poem was not well reviewed.

Cullen's poem places Keats as Endymion. The poem was written after Cullen visited Keats's grave on his first trip abroad. "To Endymion" is a defense of Keats and his poem. Cullen responds to Keats's epitaph, "Here lies One Whose Name was writ in Water." He felt the poet deserved more credit for Keats's life and work in general, as well as for the poem specifically. Written in **heroic couplets** like Keats's, Cullen's poem is driven by its surface-level argument: that Keats deserves more praise. Unlike the earlier poem praising Keats, this one has little to offer the reader. There is no insight, mature or naïve. The language is not remarkable, and the subject is uninteresting in the way it is written.

Copper Sun is full of these kinds of disappointments for readers. While many critics and peers chided him for not writing more about race, the most valid argument against the book is that it is simply uninteresting. It shows no depth or growth for the poet.

THE BLACK CHRIST AND OTHER POEMS (1929)

The title poem of *The Black Christ* is one of Cullen's most damning criticisms of race in the United States. The poem is dedicated to white America. It follows two brothers wrestling with their Christian faith. It is written in two parts and is narrated by the older brother. The first part preaches about the shame of the country, racism, and how the older brother has seen God's glory. He urges the reader to be open to beauty and faith.

The second part is the story that led to the older brother's reaffirmed faith. It opens with a recitation from his mother. She describes the beauty of the spring, and her attachment—as a black woman—to the land of the South, despite its cruelty. Unlike the rich white women, she has worked the land and knows and loves it well. She doesn't pay mind to the suffering because she has her sights on the promise of heaven. When the brothers are alone, Jim, the younger of the two, challenges his mother's beliefs. He wonders why a merciful God would let black people suffer racism. Perhaps, he wonders ruefully, God thinks these injustices are deserved. He then dismisses the existence of God entirely. The older brother is stuck in the middle. He sympathizes with Jim but does not want to hurt his mother.

Jim grows into a handsome man. He is described as the cool, dark night after a long, hot day. The townspeople notice his beauty and pride and disdain him for it. Both brothers fear that Jim may get into trouble if he can't keep a low profile. Though they all sense the danger, their mother refuses to leave the South. She has, in the older brother's words, nailed them there.

One night, the older brother finds Jim bleeding from his head. Jim tells him that he had an affair with a white woman. A white man caught them. The white man struck him and (possibly) the woman, and Jim fought back. Jim killed the man and is now on the run from a mob. The older brother hides Jim, and tries to get the mob to leave the house. Instead, they grab Jim and take him out to a nearby tree to be lynched.

At the end of the poem, Jim rises again in front of his brother, reaffirming their faith. The family prays and weeps together. They leave the South to live with some security, and they praise God.

The poem is starkly different from Cullen's previous work. While it retains the same meter, end rhyme, and themes of other poems, the language is richer, deeper, and more layered.

Lint Shaw Shot to Death by mob
Colbert, Ga. April 28, 1936

"The Jury Finds The Deceased Came To His
Death at the Hands of Parties Unknown"

"The Sheriff Reported He Was Unable To
Recognize Anyone at The Scene of The Lynching"

Though the faces are clearly visible in the photo, the lynch mob was not served justice. The note on the photo explains the reason behind the all too common story.

One such passage is when Jim describes what happened with the white woman. Entrenched in the beauty of the spring, he says, their two souls found one another. So enraptured by this beauty, they fell in love. Their mother had described the beauty of spring through the land. But Jim saw the beauty of spring in love. The white woman is conflated with the beauty of the spring and its intoxication. When the white man berates her and pulls her by her hair, she cannot react. Jim says the blows he took did not hurt as badly as the words that had lashed her. While physical wounds can heal, words linger, leaving the recipient half dead, half alive.

Both Jim and his mother value beauty; however, their reactions to its destruction are different. With the beauty of spring dead, Jim reacts violently. When beautiful Jim is lynched, the mother reacts by praying. It is clear which reaction Cullen favors in the end.

At its climax, the poem is raw and emotional. The most emotional passage is the strongest in the poem. Jim has been carried off by the mob to be hanged, and his mother is on her knees crying and praying. The older brother, pained that he could not save Jim, becomes furious with his mother's prayers. He coldly mocks her, saying she may pray to her God and he will pray to a stone. Then they can see whose prayer is answered first. He accuses Jesus Christ of being a racist, disdainful of God's dark creatures. He demands to know, from the rock, why someone as beautiful as Jim had to die.

The outburst of human emotion and the fixation on beauty keeps the poem from being preachy. Though the outcome of the poem goes back to Cullen's Christian upbringing, it is the tension in the older brother's despair that gives the most damning picture of what racism has done to black people. God and faith are symbols of hope for an oppressed people. When overcome by suffering, hope is something to be disdained because, for so long, it never changed anything.

The poem, while problematic in many ways, is a reminder of Cullen's poetic talent. However, it did little to stem the tide against his fading star.

THE MEDEA AND SOME POEMS (1935)

Aside from Cullen's translation of the Greek play, the book features twenty-seven poems, including four translations and ten sonnets. Most of the poems are darker than his previous works. They are full of death, despair, lost love, and feelings of hopelessness. The sonnets in particular string together a story of love lost and pride.

The poem that gained the most attention is the last, "Scottsboro, Too, Is Worth Its Song." Dedicated to American poets, it laments the silence around the case of the Scottsboro Boys. In 1931, nine black teenagers were accused of raping two white teenagers on a train. Five of the boys were sentenced to life in prison. Due to the hastiness of the trials, the lack of evidence, conflicting testimonies, and racial bias of the jury, the case was a prime example of a miscarriage of justice. There was a demonstration in Harlem, but Cullen thought the efforts were not enough.

In the poem, Cullen calls on American poets to speak about the Scottsboro case. The poem argues that the case should have penetrated the heart of America's artists. They should have written about it like they do their other enemies: disease, death, and war. Artists, he writes in the poem, had taken up the case of two Italian-Americans, Sacco and Vanzetti, who were falsely accused of a crime. They should have had songs for the Scottsboro Boys, too. He ends the poem wondering why artists have not taken up the cry.

The poem is weak in language. The thought is not terribly profound. Nor is there any surprising element along the way. The implicit answer to his question is obvious, though it is meant to be so. Instead the poem preaches, but without any of the heart or talent Cullen's readers had been accustomed to.

A white crowd cheers at the trial of the Scottsboro Boys, in which black teens were convicted with little evidence in a speedy trial.

As his last book of poetry, it was a far cry from his better works in *Color* and *The Black Christ and Other Poems*. His poetic strengths were in image and challenging perceptions. When he challenged his own sentiments, as he did in "The Black Christ," there was a raw emotional quality to the otherwise sterile meters of his work. Whether it was due to the negative reviews or personal pressure, Cullen turned away from poetry to pursue prose and plays.

CHAPTER FIVE

A CURIOUS THING

large part of Countee Cullen's legacy is the reactions he elicited from critics. Praised for his first book, critics and fans had high expectations for Cullen's future work. However, his later works brought mixed reviews and controversy. A combination of things led to his work falling away. For one thing, critics and artists were divided on where race stood in terms of art and what the artist owed to his or her race. With widespread disagreement on this issue, Cullen was sure to face criticism for his approach to race issues. In addition, his lack of growth—especially in form— earned him criticism. Critics wanted to see Cullen do something new and exciting with his work. Cullen's productivity suffered, and with little new work, he could not recover his status among his peers. Meanwhile, the Great Depression greatly reduced the white audience for black literature and art. As a result, Cullen had a more limited audience and fewer opportunities.

Indeed, many historians cite the Great Depression as the end of the Harlem Renaissance, though others extend it to the beginning of World War II. By the time *The Black Christ and Other*

Opposite: Cullen's portrait captures a thoughtful expression as he looks off in the distance, perhaps thinking of what lies ahead.

Poems was published, the literary landscape had changed drastically. The Harlem Renaissance had heavily relied on a white audience, white patrons, and white establishments. The Great Depression disrupted the demand for black art. White patrons were more concerned with their own financial issues. Losing the audience—and therefore the demand—for their work, black artists were hit harder than their white counterparts. In turn, critics looked less favorably on racial art. Whether this was due to the Great Depression or to their own circumstances, critics were quick to declare that Harlem was no longer in vogue. Black artists were still finding praise and success, but it was less widespread than before. Only a lucky few maintained the good favor of critics and patrons. Cullen was not so fortunate. While trying to find work to stay afloat, he also tried to navigate a new literary landscape. Where the doors were once open for black literature, they were steadily closing. Critics ultimately turned away from Cullen.

In some ways it was to be expected. Cullen's later work did not live up to expectations, so when he did produce a poem of particular skill, the critics had already turned a blind eye. This fact, coupled with a big decrease in the number of poems he was writing, meant there was less opportunity for Cullen to assert himself.

One frequent complaint against his work was that he never developed his own worldview. While it is true he had no unique insight, his contradictions were not the signal of a thoughtless mind. The idea that Cullen did not have a worldview is absurd when taking in the body of his work and its themes.

However, one significant point against Cullen's work was that he did not change with the poetic landscape. His language was too archaic for the times, and he never developed a style of his own. Critics believed that reading his poems for form was a futile exercise, because there would be little to learn.

In 1947, critic Harvey Curtis Webster warned poets to look at Cullen as an example of a promising poet not adapting to the

Keats was one of the biggest poetic influences for Cullen.

artistic landscape and the dangers of not receiving constructive criticism. He believed Cullen had been surrounded by unearned praise. Webster said that black intellectuals had wanted to promote one of their own, and white patrons, not wanting to appear bigoted, had supported him. This idea flies in the face of the criticism Cullen did receive in reviews. However, by analyzing his poetry, it is clear that he did not apply any of the criticisms to his craft. Nor did he apply his criticisms of other artists to his own poetic growth.

DELVING INTO *COLOR* (1925)

When *Color* was published in 1925, Cullen was only twenty-two years old. The poems were vibrant and strengthened by Cullen's peculiar insights into issues. His youth and talent drew more attention to the possibilities of his future than the virtues of his verse. George H. Dillon, a critic from *Poetry* magazine, praised Cullen's writing. However, he also noted that Cullen was apt to use awkward phrasing to keep the structure sound, rather than use a more common expression. Helen Keller, noted activist and writer, said the book was full of youthful emotions, though she said little in the way of specifics. Cullen would later write a poem for her.

In regard to race, critics had varying opinions on the more racial poems, such as "Incident." This was the beginning of the battle over Cullen's thoughts on race. Though he held some nuanced views, they would be lost for some time while artists, activists, and civil rights leaders argued about racial politics.

EXPLORING *COPPER SUN* (1927)

Copper Sun was a moderate success for Cullen. Critics saw that this collection had more depth than *Color*. Some of the poetry was certainly more mature than his previous book. He had also refrained from using as many awkward phrases. He was again

Helen Keller was a formidable critic, feminist, and political activist. Cullen shared a brief correspondence with her after she praised his first book.

praised and condemned for his use of race in his poetry. Some critics, such as Herman Gorman, believed Cullen was transcending the arena of race to embrace universal ideas. But others, such as Harry Alan Potamkin, believed Cullen was exploiting issues of race. The fact that race was a pivotal point for critics infuriated Cullen. It was around this time when he tried to move away from *Color* onto other pursuits.

AS EDITOR OF *CAROLING DUSK* (1927)

Cullen's solid publishing history helped secure him a deal to be the editor of an anthology of verse by black poets in 1927. At this time, he was still receiving accolades for his first book, though it had been published two years earlier. As the anthology editor, he had an expansive approach to gleaning artists' work. He used his connections to gather a multitude of writing. His friend Langston Hughes had collected work from Aquah LaLuah, a member of the Fanti tribe in Africa who lived in England. Its inclusion in Cullen's anthology showed his view that blackness was a diaspora not limited to the United States. Cullen also secured work from more established poets like Claude McKay, Langston Hughes, and others. He even included a verse by an eight-year-old girl.

Critics felt that Cullen had allowed too much in the anthology. He accepted writing that was not of a high caliber. Perhaps to many critics it was just another instance in which his lack of a worldview haunted him. For Cullen, however, the anthology was less about the work in question and more about proving a point. He used the anthology to show the diversity of black poets. No one who read it would retain the idea that black poetry was solidified and unchanging. The response, however, was lukewarm at best. People had hoped to see writing that excited them. While there were certainly many poems and poets who did, by including work that Cullen knew was of a low caliber, he had disappointed readers. His selections had more to do with his desire to break out of what was thought to be "Negro poetry" than they did with quality writing.

NOTICING "THE BALLAD OF THE BROWN GIRL" (1927)

"The Ballad of the Brown Girl" drew notice when it won second place in the Witter Bynner undergraduate poetry contest in 1923. A leading expert on literary ballads, Dr. Lyman Kittredge of Harvard University called the poem one of the best ballads he had ever read. Some critics, though, disdained Cullen's poem for his racializing of the original ballad by making the Brown Girl a black woman. Critics also accused him of a racial misreading of the original poem. However, the overall reception was highly positive and the poem is a must-read for those looking to understand Cullen's work.

A CHANGE WITH *THE BLACK CHRIST AND OTHER POEMS* (1929)

The Black Christ and Other Poems is a small book with twenty-four poems in addition to the longer narrative title poem. The collection is Cullen's third volume of poetry. Themes of departure, unrequited love, loss, and death surfaced alongside racial themes. Cullen's work had finally shown the maturity critics were hoping to see in *Copper Sun*. The themes were darker and he championed a worldview centered on religious faith and destiny.

Though the book was a stark contrast to Cullen's earlier work, critics still believed he had not matured artistically. The aesthetic of his poetry had not changed much. His persistent use of classical poetry forms effectively masked any growth in his themes.

A QUESTION OF AESTHETICS

Cullen's affinity for the Romantic poets has only been speculated about. He did not appear to mind that he was writing in a form that did not match his time. The early praise seemed to agree with him. When a college professor read one of Cullen's poems to a class, the students believed the writer had lived at the same time as Keats or Shelley. They were surprised to discover that the poet was a contemporary writer. This fact undoubtedly pleased Cullen, but it did not bode well for his longevity among the public readership. That his craft changed so little was considered a great disservice to his writing life. Critics were quick to say he had not matured. They did not, however, have any ideas about what maturity would look like for a writer like Cullen.

While some missteps were easy to identify, such as the awkward phrasing, it seemed that critics were just tired of Cullen's form. However, this does not indicate a lack of maturity. Cullen had matured greatly as an individual, but he had chosen not to write in that voice. When he did write more maturely in his last few works, critics were still not appeased. The archaic language and unimaginative meters masked any growth in the content of his poetry—the packaging being uninteresting.

By this point, Cullen had more detractors than fans. He had more negative reviews than positive. Critic Granville Hicks said that Cullen's skills were not developing, though he did not state specifics.

The Harlem Renaissance disappeared practically overnight. Because of the Great Depression, race was no longer the hot issue; now it was the economy. Writers like John Steinbeck, William Faulkner, and detective novelist Dashiell Hammett became popular. In poetry, readers sought refuge in verse by such poets as Wallace Stevens, Robert Frost, and William Carlos Williams. And it's apt to point out that most of these poets wrote in metered lines with rhyme (though not with Cullen's archaic language). By this point, Cullen had lost the critics and the audience for his work.

RECEIVING *ONE WAY TO HEAVEN* (1932)

Cullen began to move forward on "a great Negro American novel." He had decided to write the book, in part, as a response to Carl Van Vechten's controversial novel *Nigger Heaven*. Van Vechten's novel drew outrage from the Harlem community, which, prior to the book's publication, had welcomed him into its inner circle of artists.

One Way to Heaven was Cullen's only novel. The characters were well developed and the prose well written. Bringing together the strength of Cullen's characters with the racial divides of the time, one critic wrote that it was strange how human the characters were. The story, however, lacked the tying threads readers were looking for. Overall, the novel was not well received.

Many critics argued that the story would have been better if it had been two separate novels. The story of lower-class Mattie and Sam as the first novel and the satire of middle-class Harlem as the other. The two storylines, after all, did not pair well. The rich Harlemites did little to advance the plot of the overall story. They therefore felt superfluous to the story. In a twist of irony, Cullen's

The disparity in economics between upper- and lower-class blacks weighed heavily in the backdrop of Cullen's novel, *One Way to Heaven*.

writing was alive and enchanting when he was describing the social world he knew so well. But these sections were of little consequence to the central story. The rest of the writing was lackluster. In the end, the novel was another disappointment for Cullen.

Contemporary critics, however, consider the novel one of the best satires of the period, particularly because of its portrayal of middle- and upper-class blacks.

INTERPRETING *THE MEDEA AND SOME POEMS* (1935)

Cullen's next venture was in his translation of *Medea*. Though it was the first translation of an ancient Greek play by a black writer, it was not given importance on that fact—nor, arguably, should it have been. Cullen chose to make the play easier to read for modern audiences. His language choices were, at first, hailed for bringing the work of Euripides into spoken English. Soon after, however, critics argued that Cullen's translation had reduced Euripides to little more than a folktale aimed at black concerns.

The fact that black concerns were considered a reduction of a classic play says more about the reviewer than it does about the play. Adapting Greek and other myths or fairy tales to modern times has always been a touchstone of Western literature. These kinds of stories have been adapted time and again as novels, plays, movies, and television shows. Often these adaptations make commentary on the current times.

Another brief review merely said the shorter poems were characteristic of Cullen's style. Though some critics later saw a newfound maturity in the poems, overall there was little interest in Cullen's latest work. His star was already beginning to fade. Dashed again, this book was the last collection of poetry that Cullen published.

Recently, *Medea* has had a resurgence in scholarly interest. Lillian Corti, in her paper "Countee Cullen's *Medea*," argues that despite its early dismissal, Cullen's translation is a subversive drama that was marred not by its own merits, but by the misfortune surrounding it.

SUCCESS WITH *THE LOST ZOO* (1940)

His next project was in children's books. *The Lost Zoo* was the first success Cullen had in a long time. Though it did not grow to become a children's classic, it gained him a young readership. The popularity of Christopher the cat—who was listed as coauthor of the book—was a large draw for children. Young readers often asked Cullen questions about the famed feline. *American Libraries* listed a new edition of the book as one of the notable children's books of 1969. Encouraged by this success, Cullen decided to write another children's book. This time Christopher Cat was the main author, in collaboration with Countee Cullen.

Scholars have looked at the children's book and wondered if it was meant to be enjoyed by adults. The book's dedication indicates to some scholars that the book was meant to be enjoyed by adults as well as children. Certain stories, such as one about a skunk who is discriminated against by the other animals on the ark, would be an obvious comment on civil rights for older readers.

MORE PROMISE WITH *MY LIVES AND HOW I LOST THEM* (1942)

My Lives and How I Lost Them appeared two years after *The Lost Zoo*. Written by Christopher Cat with help from Cullen, the book focused on the various lives of Christopher. The book's charm came from the interplay between Cullen and his cat, Christopher. Christopher relays the story to his owner with sarcasm, sass, wit, and humor. Interspersed with the various stories are Christopher's insights into humanity and cat society. He declares where they are similar and where they disagree. Additionally, Christopher makes the case for antidiscrimination and antiracism when he argues against "speciesism," which seeks to prevent him and other animals from writing or fulfilling other dreams.

Critics were not as impressed with this book as they were with the last one. Arguably not as imaginative and more cautious, Cullen's second and last children's book was still a measured success.

THE CONTROVERSIAL *ST. LOUIS WOMAN* (1946)

Cullen's attempt at adapting Arna Bontemps's novel *God Sends Sunday* as a Broadway musical was perhaps the biggest endeavor of his literary career. The project required him to travel frequently, work in a team, and adhere to tough deadlines.

Though the project seemed promising, it was steeped in controversy. One problem was that the story was not emotionally uplifting. It ended with the main character running away to Mexico in order to escape murder charges. This was not a typical ending for a Broadway musical. Working with Bontemps, and later Langston Hughes, the writers juggled the expectations of agents, producers, and audiences.

In 1943, an outburst of controversy surrounded the contents of the script. The controversy concerned racial uplift. Black leaders in the community disdained the types of black characters portrayed in the show. Pimps, prostitutes, gamblers, and unwed parents were considered as too low for the aspirations of the New Negro. Though the idea of the New Negro was by now decades old, it still lingered in the circles of the black bourgeoisie.

Cullen's use of these characters flew in the face of his reception as a New Negro figure. The characters would, they argued, further cement the stereotypes the Harlem Renaissance had fought hard to dispel.

That the show was marred by controversy before it was even staged left a huge shadow over the entire enterprise. Walter White and Lena Horne led the negative press. Horne had previously been slated to play the love interest to the lead character. Cullen took their protests personally. Despite his best efforts, the tongue-lashing would not stop. When the show finally premiered, the musical ran for one hundred and thirteen shows.

Arna Bontemps, originally from California, was drawn to the bustling activity of the Harlem Renaissance, where he would begin a successful career and become close friends with Cullen.

ON THESE I STAND (1947)

While only containing a small number of new poems, *On These I Stand* is a fascinating look at how Cullen evaluated his own body of work. He had put together this collection to feature what he believed to be his best poetry. Putting an editorial eye to his own writing, he cut many poems from *Color*, which was considered his most successful book. More than half of the poems in *Color* were cut from the collection. Cullen also let go of thirty-seven poems from *Copper Sun*, twenty-two from *The Black Christ and Other Poems*, and eight from *The Medea and Some Poems*.

The fact that he dispelled with most of the poems from *Color* is a curious thing. Though critics believed his first book to be his best, it seems the poet did not share their opinion. Some of his most quoted poems, such as "Atlantic City Waiter," did not make the cut. Perhaps the shadow of that book's success had left him with a feeling of resentment toward it. Cullen also cut most of his witty epitaphs and juvenilia poems. The poems that he did include were not poems most readers would think of as his best work.

In his review of *On These I Stand*, Harvey Curtis Webster was disappointed that more passages from *The Lost Zoo* weren't included. He was also disdainful of some of Cullen's previously unpublished works, such as "Dear Friends and Gentle Hearts."

It was clear from the collection that Cullen saw himself and his work differently from how critics and fans viewed him. Due to the surprising omissions and inclusions of what he considered his greatest pieces, critics were quick to ascertain meaning. The collection became a symbol of how Cullen's potential never came to full fruition.

A DIFFICULT CAREER

At the beginning of Countee Cullen's career, the reception for his work started out friendly, but this did not last long. Without

The Great Depression was a difficult time in the United States, and it shifted the nation's cultured focus away from the Harlem Renaissacne.

the support or approval of key figures and critics, Cullen's work faded from the public's mind. Though the process was slow, by the twenty-first century, more schools were teaching Langston Hughes than were citing Cullen.

After *Copper Sun* received an unenthusiastic reception, the arc of Cullen's career was on a downward slope. A multitude of external and personal factors led to his waning career, not least of which was his inability to make good on the promise set by *Color*.

Cullen was a mystery to his contemporaries and critics. At times, what he said in interviews seemed to contradict his own poetic practices. While he said that black poets must turn away from writing about race, he wrote about race extensively. For a poet who seemed to have no worldview, he had many messages to spread. People speculated on why Cullen was drawn to an old aesthetic, but no one knew for sure why he was compelled to write the way he did.

The greatest disappointment from Cullen's body of work was that there was no sense of artistic growth. Though Cullen the man matured, Cullen the poet seemed to stay more or less the same, especially with regard to his aesthetic.

Moreover, the devastation of the Great Depression left little room on the public stage for black writers. Even in the Harlem Renaissance, black writers had a hard time compared to their white colleagues. Those artists like Cullen who had not stepped up in growth or popularity fell by the wayside.

That Cullen's poetry fell out of favor so soon in his career seemed a testament to his worth as a poet. His plays, novel, and children's books were overlooked as well, though this was in part because his fame was derived from his poetry.

With Cullen, critics and readers found more questions than answers. Much like his earlier life, there are still many things left to understand about the poet.

Cullen's legacy is difficult to determine. It could simply be that he was a poet, black, and able to sing at a riveting historical time that elevated him beyond his poetic merits. His writing, however, has yet to be unpacked fully. Renewed scholarship, fresh insights, and continued research of Cullen's life and work will show if his work truly stands the test of time.

CHAPTER SIX

HEAR HIM SING

Once called the poet laureate of the Harlem Renaissance, Countee Cullen enjoyed only a short-lived career. His popularity waned soon after the publication of his first book of poetry. He was dubbed the poet laureate because of his breakout premiere in both black and white circles, as well as his position of esteem with influential people. A poet laureate, by definition, writes poems for special occasions and oversees events that promote literary arts.

In some ways, Cullen filled this role for the Harlem Renaissance. As the assistant editor of *Opportunity*, he promoted black writers. He also wrote poems for specific occasions, such as the Scottsboro Boys case. However, the position at *Opportunity* only lasted two years, and as time went on, he wrote less and less poetry of his own.

The unofficial title, in some ways, kept Cullen in the spotlight when he otherwise might have faded away. His attitude toward race was not seen favorably at the time. His penchant for beauty was undervalued. And his archaic writing style was never balanced with any unique invention.

Opposite: One of the main draws of the Harlem Renaissance was the enticing jazz music. Legendary musicians would get their start on the stages in Harlem.

Some of his contemporaries, such as Langston Hughes, withstood time better than Cullen. The success of these writers further proved that there was no place in modern black literature for this black poet who wrote like a white Romantic. Cullen's ideas about race fell into a grey area that people could not rally behind and hold up as an example for others.

There are heavy shadows cast on Cullen's legacy. The years of **negritude, Black Power,** and the **Black Arts movement** did not embrace Cullen's work. Various fads in black art came in and out of favor during his career. At one point, it was considered favorable to assert black people's Americanness, as Du Bois preferred. Later, the arts movement favored asserting black people's blackness. Cullen stood in the middle. He was conflicted about these approaches. It showed in his work, and he quickly lost support from critics. Hughes's infamous criticism that Cullen wrote white because he wanted to be white was forever damaging to Cullen's legacy.

From the almost infamous article by Margaret Sperry of the *Brooklyn Daily Eagle*, biographers have fixated on one feature. On the issue of race, Cullen said, he wanted to be a poet, not a Negro poet. He repeated this sentiment to his friends, most notably to Hughes.

From a cursory glance, this statement seems like the dismissal of his race. Many biographers have latched onto it fiercely in that regard. Cullen's statement is used to promote a kind of colorblindness in interpreting his work. But this viewpoint absolves the reader of seeing an important part of who Cullen was. The statement is sometimes also used to create a false opposition between Hughes and Cullen. However, in both these cases, an examination of Cullen's poetry is missing. There is a good deal more to know of Countee Cullen through reading his poetry than there is from reading a simple statement about not wanting to be known only as a Negro poet.

This notion that a person is not entirely his or her race is not new. It was not new when Cullen expressed it, or when Martin

Luther King Jr. described his dream. Even today, poets resist these kinds of labels. Labeling artists based on their race can be very limiting. Some of their experiences can be viewed through a lens of their race, but they are also creating work based on the universal human experience, which everyone should be able to relate to. Yet, the idea did not catch on in Harlem, where black was in vogue. Scholars and artists were scrambling to decide what being black meant, both in society and in the art world.

To Cullen, the poet's job is to describe experiences that expose beauty and truth. Part of this is race, language, and culture. But other parts include things like the loveliness of spring and quiet conversations with a loved one.

Cullen was more driven by beauty through image than any other facet of poetry. The compulsion did not translate to the work of line or form. His aesthetic never truly changed. However, his best-loved poems, and those with critical acclaim, relied heavily on image and emotion.

When Cullen rejected art as merely a form of propaganda, he was making room for his real muse: beauty. As time went on, the public grew less enamored with this view. They became impatient to see him mature or evolve.

Waiting for Cullen to evolve would prove difficult for most critics. He faced many pressures on all sides of his life. Cullen was raised by a Christian reverend, but he had pagan and possibly homosexual desires. He was part of the upper-class Harlemite society, which dictated how he should conduct himself. He had many people telling him whom it was suitable for him to marry. Also, he lived in a racist society that continually erupted around him.

Cullen's aesthetic clouded any growth he may have undergone. His use of awkward, archaic language and phrasing further obscured what he was trying to accomplish in his writing. His poems started to sound too similar to each other. Critics and readers felt that they had read all this before. There was nothing new in Cullen's his work that excited them.

Cullen may also have been stunted by the early praise he received. He was encouraged to pursue his poetry, partly because of his talent, but also because of what a young black poet symbolized for the black community. When he did receive criticism, Cullen he did not always apply it to his work.

Still, Cullen would continue to be called the poet laureate long after his death. Hughes would be known, jokingly, as the poet "low-reate," further emphasizing the opposite ends of the spectrum that these poets occupied.

Cullen did little to promote the Harlem Renaissance. The movement was at the cross section of race and art. But even though Cullen was part of the Harlem Renaissance, he resented the mention of race in his interviews. Cullen was more interested in the idea of beauty than any of the racial aspects the Renaissance sought to promote. He resented the idea that his only artistic purpose was racial uplift.

Given his meteoric rise and long, drawn-out fall, many have found it hard to characterize Cullen's life and work. Was he simply a mediocre poet who happened to be in the right place at the right time? If he had not been adopted by Reverend Cullen and instead remained with his grandparents, would he still have ended up as the poet laureate? When Cullen came to live with the reverend, he was able to attend more prestigious schools and meet notable black leaders. What would have become of him if not for these opportunities?

Overall, Cullen's contemporaries believed he was not concerned enough with race in content or character. The ideas he shared on race have been scathingly reduced. His poetry was too far behind in terms of aesthetics for modern audiences. Readers preferred free verse. Cullen was outdated.

Initially, critics thought Cullen was locked in the past because of the kind of poetry he wrote. Cullen was in an odd predicament. His sensibilities about the place of black artists were more suited to the twenty-first century, which was decades away, but his poetic style was of the nineteenth century. He was a man out of time. In today's society, it would have been much easier find people who agree with his assessment of how race relates to art.

Cullen had grown up in America during World War I and the years of industrialization. People were struggling to understand their place in the world. People were moving away from rural farm life to the cities. Factories churned out goods to be sold across the country and abroad. But while America was coming into a new identity, it was also limited. Segregation, racism, and sexism had cut out large groups of people from the chance to be a part of the new America. Black writers tried to determine what it meant to be black, American, and artists. Prior to the Harlem Renaissance, blacks were encouraged to assimilate to white standards. Many black artists rejected this idea. Instead, they sought to define a genuinely black identity.

Cullen's work can be seen as an attempt to bridge the gap between white and black Americans. For centuries, blacks had been denied citizenship and the right to call themselves Americans. Ultimately, however, Cullen chose to abandon all labels aside from that of "poet." This was not because he did not find importance in those labels—they permeated his art constantly—but Cullen found that no matter the label, it could be used to limit the artistic spirit. He saw himself as a black man and an artist, just not a "black artist."

Today, the question of identity is even more complex. Due in part to advances in communication, we are all part of a global community, but discussions about identity still take place. From the arguments against racist mascots to the exploration of self-pride, the question of identity covers all areas of life.

In recent years, Cullen's poetry has been revived. In April 2015, in response to the Baltimore uprising against police brutality, poet Jericho Brown wrote an article for the Poetry Foundation. He described the mainstream media's failure to report the situation. Brown's letter to CNN's Wolf Blitzer featured Cullen's poem

"Incident." The ninety-year-old poem was still relevant, emotional, and ultimately powerful. It spoke to the frustrations of black people in Baltimore and all across America. Cullen's poetry is still anthologized and studied to varying degrees today.

Perhaps Cullen's greatest legacy was being a part of the great conversations around him. He gave voice to a view that was not popular among his contemporaries. But this point of view may have more importance today.

THE RACIAL MOUNTAIN

Cullen's legacy has always been compared to the work and legacy of his contemporary and friend Langston Hughes. The poets represent two sides of the same coin. Critics view them as champions of different subsets of the Harlem Renaissance. Cullen was the paragon of the New Negro. He was part of the Talented Tenth and, therefore, a symbol of the aspirations of bourgeois black people. He represented middle-class Harlemites and intellectuals. Hughes, with his bluesy music and folkish idioms, was the leader of working-class black people. His work made their issues, lives, and culture beautiful. Cullen helped to bring black people into mainstream white America. His work assimilated with white culture and adopted European poetic forms. Hughes, on the other hand, aligned himself with the more radical side. His poetry brought an originality to black art. His was considered an authentically black aesthetic.

This contrast was famously examined in Hughes's own essay "The Negro Artist and the Racial Mountain," published in the *Nation* in 1926. The essay, however, clouds the nuance that Cullen actually held in his viewpoint on race. The essay is a thinly veiled slight against Cullen, greatly oversimplifying Cullen's viewpoints on race.

Hughes pulled no punches when he wrote that one of the most promising of black poets of the times told him he does not

Despite the at times fierce competition between them, Cullen and Langston Hughes remained friends. Cullen had even urged Hughes, pictured here, to finish his degree.

want to be a black poet. Hughes asserted that because this poet didn't want to be a black poet and wrote like a white poet, it meant he subconsciously wanted to be a white person.

It is unfair and unrealistic to mask Cullen's ideas on race and art in such an inflammatory way. Still, this essay is often cited when discussing his legacy on race. Biographer Blanch E. Ferguson thought that the proportion of Cullen's poems on racial issues was proof of his desire to not be seen as a racial poet. (Ferguson's research, however, is considered unreliable as a source on Cullen's life.) Later biographers believed that Cullen disavowed the importance of race in his writing life. He is most frequently quoted on this subject based on an interview he gave in a newspaper article titled "Countee P. Cullen, Negro Boy Poet, Tells His Story." He tells journalist Margaret Sperry that he does not want to be regarded as a black poet. However, that stands in stark contrast to his most quoted lines from his poem "Yet Do I Marvel."

Throughout his life, Cullen repeatedly sought to clarify his stance on race, but it was to no avail. His ideas had been reduced to a few ill-chosen quotations. Though his ideas were more nuanced than he was given credit for, few people were interested in the truth. For whatever reason, people were unwilling to hear him.

It is not for a lack of trying on Cullen's part. Even in the Sperry article, he went on to say that America's fascination with race has hindered black artists. Black artists focused on race to gain acceptance. It became their one trick and they were not able to move past it. Cullen went on to affirm that writing about race is not something a poet who is black should refrain from doing. Of course, if poets write from experience and emotions and they happen to be black, those racial experiences are going to turn into poems. When the emotion is there, he says, the poet must express it.

Cullen's concern was twofold. He did not want to be in service to propaganda, even if it was for racial uplift. He did not want to become limited in what he could say. He thought that pigeonholing black poets to issues of race meant that black artists would not be able to take part in conversations about universal ideas. He did not think that these universal ideas should be a topic that only white artists could write about. At the time, being white meant one's concerns could be universal. White people, being considered a standard, were seen as enlightened enough not to be swayed by racial biases. It was the same line of reasoning that sought to delegitimize concerns of women. Women were thought to be too emotional to have universal ideas about society and people of color were thought to be too primitive minded.

Even today, critics sometimes believe that the experiences of white people are more universal than other races. The logic that follows is that black poetry is primarily about social justice. Any non–social justice poetry, then, is not black poetry. But this implies that all other forms of poetry are, in fact, white poetry. It is a poor argument. Of course, black artists have as much right to express the full scope of the human experience. What's more, white people can and do write social protest poetry. It is not a form that only belongs to black poets.

What this means is not a total disavowal of race or its importance. The Harlem Renaissance fought against the black buffoon stereotype. In their resistance, there was the question of a new aesthetic, like Hughes proposed, and assimilation, like Du Bois proposed. Cullen, though, fell in the middle. His poems routinely assert the uniqueness and exceptionalism of African people, though he wrote in a European style.

LITERATURE AND IDENTITY

Cullen's personal history helps researchers better understand his beliefs on identity. He grew up in Harlem with an activist father who was the head of the largest congregation in the area. Great black leaders surrounded him growing up. He heard stories of racial injustices all across America. It was enough to make him at one time—as he admitted to a friend—hate white people.

At school, his classmates were mostly white. His teachers were all white. But having been very successful in his school career, it seems unlikely that he faced much discrimination (though one can only speculate). Cullen's love of poetry and his first taste of poetic success were directly tied to his attending majority white schools. The poetry he read, aside from Dunbar, was mostly by white people. His biggest influence was Keats, a white poet. Where his poetic preference came from is nothing to wonder at.

By attending white schools and finding success in them, Cullen must have felt a level of ownership of Romantic white artists. Within the poetic forms that he read and loved, he proved that a black poet could write as well as any white one. While he wondered about what he had gained from his African heritage (most notably in the poem "Heritage"), his comfort with his white inheritance is clear.

Cullen did not shy away from his race or the experiences of it, but he refused to be defined by it. Ideally, he would have wanted to be held to the same standards as any poet, regardless of race. He wanted the language to speak for itself. He rejected having been defined as an outsider in American literature.

In the foreword of *Caroling Dusk*, Cullen made a case for poetry by blacks being classified as American poetry. He called the anthology one of verse by black poets, instead of black verse. To him, "black verse" implied there was only one kind of black poetry. "Verse by black poets," on the other hand, asserted that black poets were just as artistically diverse as white poets. Cullen said that black artists have inherited the English language and its artistic history just the same as white artists. African Americans are, after all, inhabitants and citizens of the United States and not a nation in Africa.

Cullen's attitude toward race and art was more in line with those of the twenty-first century, rather than the twentieth century. Like him, many current writers reject the ghettoization of their work. Writers like Toni Morrison echoed these sentiments on *The Colbert Report* with Stephen Colbert, among other venues. When Colbert asked her about resisting the label of "African American writer" and what she would want to be labeled instead, she responded, "An American writer."

Black writers today do not want their work set aside in just one space. It is unfair that the privilege of being an American writer is only for white, male artists. Even when special attention is made to help promote one group or another, in doing so we are limiting those artists to that one space. Schools in particular often function this way. Black writers are often taught only in February as part of Black History Month, if they are taught at all.

Cullen did not want to be limited to one place in the literary landscape. This attitude was revolutionary on his part. At the time, black Americans were not just being relegated to certain places in their art but also in their waking life. Businesses did not hire

The rights of black people were often denied or trampled on. The obstacles facing blacks trying to vote would be part of the civil rights movement decades later.

or serve them. Some sections of the country were completely off limits to blacks. Political discussion of race was often hostile toward black Americans. How, then, could Cullen expect to be held up as an equal to white poets in America?

In the end, his forward thinking did him a disservice. History celebrated Langston Hughes but dismissed Cullen. Years later,

THE POSTHUMOUS COMING OUT

The issue of Cullen's sexuality has resurged in recent years. It is widely accepted among scholars that he was attracted to men. This acceptance has galvanized readings of his poetry. Sexuality has become a major theme coded into the fabric of his writing. Only a few poems have been examined repeatedly for hints of sexuality. In those poems that involve sexual desire, Cullen may have substituted women in place of men. His poetry involves the beautifying of men. He laments the loss of beauty when Jim is lynched in "The Black Christ" and describes the passionate sway of the "Atlantic City Waiter."

As the son of a reverend, Cullen's sexuality would likely have been well hidden in his poetry. Being highly regarded by great figures such as W. E. B. Du Bois would also have given Cullen reason to hide his sexuality. Certainly the stress of his first wedding and marriage give insight into how much pressure he faced from straight black men in society. This fact makes the reading of his work even more difficult. It is likely that Cullen hid his sexuality even more deeply than perhaps his gay contemporaries.

With the economic crash, Harlem became a ghetto. Members of the Harlem Renaissance moved out, leaving the once promising place behind.

Hughes said that had the term negritude been used earlier, Cullen would have been regarded as an original negritude poet. Unfortunately, by then the effect of Hughes's essay had won out. This admission came too late to bolster what was left of Cullen's career.

Recent scholarship has begun to repair the image of Cullen's ideas on race. It certainly has helped that ideas of race and artists of color have changed over time. Historians have begun to study **intersectionality**, or the overlapping of different systems of oppression such as racism, sexism, and classism. This idea has allowed people to embrace all the different facets of their identities. Groups are able to build bridges where it was once difficult. They work together to create positive change. Cullen was a black poet, an American poet, and possibly a gay poet. He wrote out of those experiences, but he is not confined to any perceived limits set by them.

ON BEAUTY, EMPATHY, AND POWER

Beauty to Cullen was a powerful, radical force. In his poetry, it could coerce someone to sing or to commit murder. It could give life or entice the lust of Lord Death. Beauty was a formidable force, and Cullen was a devotee. His affinity for beauty may have come from his admiration for Romanticism and Romantic poets.

It may be a reach to say Cullen's attention to beauty influenced the modern landscape, but we can assess how he has been a part of the conversation. Art is, after all, a conversation. It may be a conversation between the artist and the audience, the artist and the muse, or the artist and the self. Contemporary writers such as environmental activist and writer Barry Lopez, novelist Marilynne Robinson, and poet Jericho Brown have spoken about beauty's power. Writing can overcome even the ugliest situations, creating something with at least a touch of beauty.

As Cullen notes in some of his poetry, however, beauty is often reduced to a trivial thing. When he writes in "To John Keats, Poet. At Spring Time" about how little others value beauty, he is writing not just about critics or other poets but about people in general. His criticism extends far and wide. In "To a Brown Boy," Cullen says not to be embarrassed by his reaction to beauty. He encourages the boy to embrace it. While the power of beauty is clear in the literature of many generations, it is also seen in history as well.

Beauty has a strange hold not only over the artistic mind but also over the minds of people everywhere. Nowhere is this clearer than in the Black Power movement of the 1960s and 1970s. At the time, images of black people as apes or grotesque savages were common. The rallying cry then became "black is beautiful." To regard oneself as a thing of beauty was revolutionary. Beauty did not just mean physical attractiveness, though that was an important part. It also meant beauty in all areas of a person, inside and out.

Having others recognize one's beauty was symbolic in Cullen's poetry. The fixation with Jim's beauty in "The Black Christ," was important because no one could deny it. In essence, no one could deny his humanity. By acknowledging his beauty, the onlooker was forced to exercise at least a small amount of empathy. Cullen's affinity for beauty was not solely about power and racial uplift—he recognized its profound power on people's hearts and minds.

Cullen's use of beauty was not always effective. Often the language was too archaic or the phrasing too awkward. He also relied on beauty for beauty's sake, which was not compelling for many readers. Often in studying poetry, readers want to know what the poet is trying to say. When it becomes clear that the poet is not making a larger point, readers are left frustrated. Jumping around mediocre writing can make the experience even more frustrating.

Writers have differing opinions on beauty and how to apply it, but the conversation is enthusiastic, layered, and not at all trivial, as it had been for Cullen. Perhaps because of the limits society placed on him as a black man, his issues did not receive careful discussion. His poetry, though still archaic for most modern tastes, is part of poetic discussions today.

A MINOR CHORD

Countee Cullen's legacy lives on. The 135th Street branch of the New York Public Library is named after Countee Culleen. Cullen also taught and influenced James Baldwin, who would go on to become a famous writer and activist himself.

COUNTEE CULLEN
1903 - 1946

AND WHEN YOUR BODY'S DEATH GIVES BIRTH
TO SOIL FOR SPRING TO CROWN,
MEN WILL NOT ASK IF THAT RARE EARTH
WAS WHITE FLESH ONCE, OR BROWN.

Cullen's tombstone perfectly captures his life and art. The modern, life-like statue of Cullen reaches out to a classical bust of himself wearing laurels.

Part of Cullen's legacy is as a thread in the tapestry of American literature. His voice is among those artists who have grappled with ideas and engaged in limitless conversations. His work was certainly part of the conversation, as evidenced by his poems' sometimes fiery dedications. This is, of course, the kind of legacy that all great artists leave behind.

Cullen left the world shrouded in as much mystery as when he came into it. His life, writing, and critical reception have served as a warning to young poets. His work has had a resurgence in scholarship and interest. The times he lived in proved more complicated than his poetry could stand. And yet, his best work remained complex and nuanced.

Today, his poetry might not appeal to modern readers as much as it once did. The poetic landscapes have changed. Free verse is more popular among contemporary writers. There is no indication that poetry will return to Cullen's Romantic aesthetic. However, just because Cullen's work is not modern does not mean it cannot be read with a level of appreciation. Modern readers still understand Keats, for example.

Still, Cullen's lack of ingenuity would mark him. His talents, though promising at first, were not developed. His editorial eye was called into question when taking account of *Caroling Dusk* and the poems selected for *On These I Stand*. Why had he allowed so many mediocre poems into his anthology? And why had he culled so many good ones from his own selected works? His inclusion of certain poems may have been part of a rebuttal against his critics. Even so, it seems that there was something Cullen had seen in those works that critics had not.

Though he had shown promise, Cullen did not live up to expectations. His best poems deserve in-depth readings and study, but his mediocre poems outweigh these poems in number. His failure to innovate or change devalued much of his work moving forward. In essence, Cullen was a minor poet with major ideas. He did not always articulate his ideas well in his creative work and often contradicted himself.

That his work is receiving a fresh look from scholars and writers today is interesting. His work still speaks to the causes and issues of race in America, despite what his critics thought of him. There is still much to admire and learn from his writing. Only time and new scholarship will tell if his star will rise again.

1903 Countee L. Porter is born May 30, possibly in Louisville, Kentucky.

1910 Beginning of Great Migration.

1911 Moves to Harlem, New York, to live with grandparents.

1914 World War I begins in Europe.

1917 Grandfather dies; United States enters World War I.

1918 Grandmother dies; moves in with Reverend Cullen and Carolyn Cullen; enters DeWitt Clinton High School; "To a Swimmer" published in *The Modern School*; "I Have a Rendezvous with Life" wins first place in a contest held by the Empire Federation Women's Club.

1922 Begins college at New York University.

1923 Wins second prize in Witter Bynner Poetry Contest for "The Ballad of the Brown Girl."

1924 Wins honorable mention in Witter Bynner Poetry Contest for "Spirit Birth."

1925 Begins graduate school at Harvard University; publishes *Color*.

1926 Graduates from Harvard; becomes assistant editor at *Opportunity*.

1927 Publishes *Copper Sun*; *Ballad of the Brown Girl*; *Caroling Dusk* (editor).

1928 Receives Guggenheim Fellowship; marries first wife, Nina Yolande Du Bois; moves to France.

1929 Publishes *The Black Christ and Other Poems*; stock market crashes; Great Depression begins.

1930 Divorces from Yolande Cullen.

1932 Publishes novel, *One Way to Heaven*; returns from France.

1934 Begins teaching English and French at Frederick Douglass Junior High School in New York City.

1935 Publishes *The Medea and Some Poems*.

1939 World War II begins in Europe.

1940 Publishes *The Lost Zoo*; marries second wife, Ida Mae Roberson.

1941 United States enters World War II.

1942 Publishes *My Lives and How I Lost Them*.

1946 Publishes one-act play *The Third Fourth of July* in *Theatre Arts*; controversy over *St. Louis Woman*; dies of uremic poisoning due to liver failure.

1947 Posthumously publishes *On These I Stand: An Anthology of the Best Poems of Countee Cullen*.

POETRY

Color (1925)
Copper Sun (1927)
The Ballad of the Brown Girl (1927)
The Black Christ and Other Poems (1929)
The Medea and Some Poems (1935)

ANTHOLOGIES

Caroling Dusk (editor, 1927)

NOVELS

One Way to Heaven (1932)

CHILDREN'S BOOKS

The Lost Zoo (1940) with Christopher Cat
My Lives and How I Lost Them (1942) with Christopher Cat

PLAYS

The Third Fourth of July (1946) one-act play with Owen Dodson
St. Louis Woman (1946) Broadway musical with Arna Bontemps

allegory A piece of writing that holds a hidden moralistic or political meaning.

antithesis A person or idea that is the direct opposite of another person or idea.

archaic Old or no longer used.

Black Arts movement The artistic wing of the Black Power movement.

Black Power movement A political and cultural movement for black institutions and pride in black culture beginning in the 1960s out of the civil rights movement.

free verse Poetry that has no rhyme or regulated meter.

Great Migration The movement of six million black people out of the South to the North and West from 1910 to 1970.

heroic couplet Two rhyming lines written in iambic pentameter.

iambic Describing a metrical foot of poetry where an unstressed syllable is followed by a stressed syllable.

Industrial Revolution A time of rapid industrial innovation and growth galvanized by the introduction of machinery.

intersectionality The interrelated nature of social categorizations such as race, sex, gender, sexuality, and ability, which overlap in systems of discrimination.

Jim Crow Laws that legalized racial segregation in the South after Reconstruction, disbanded in 1965.

metaphor A physical object used to represent an abstract concept.

meter Poetic beats, consisting of a number of stressed or unstressed syllables, which create music, also known as rhythm.

miscegenation The mixing of the races.

National Association for the Advancement of Colored People A civil rights organization established in 1909.

negritude The affirmation of the value of black culture, heritage, or identity.

New Negro movement A movement to resist Jim Crow laws, emphasizing racial pride and expression, but through the assimilation with white standards of conduct and culture.

Reconstruction Era The aftermath of the Civil War when Union troops were posted around the South to enforce the new freedom of enslaved people.

Romantic Describing an artistic and literary movement from the eighteenth and nineteenth centuries.

slant rhymes Words that almost rhyme phonetically. Also called half rhymes.

stanza A verse, or group of lines of a poem, separated from other lines or stanzas by white space.

Talented Tenth The designated leadership class of black people, as espoused by W. E. B. Du Bois and others.

theme The overarching subject of a poem.

FURTHER INFORMATION

BOOKS

Baker, Houston A., Jr. *A Many-Colored Coat of Dreams: The Poetry of Countee Cullen*. Detroit, MI: Broadside Press, 1974.

Haskins, Jim. *The Harlem Renaissance*. Brookfield, CT: The Millbrook Press, 1996.

Huggens, Nathan Irvin. *Harlem Renaissance*. Updated Edition. New York: Oxford University Press, 2007.

Lewis, David Levering. *When Harlem Was in Vogue*. New York: Penguin Books, 1997.

Molesworth, Charles. *And Bid Him Sing: A Biography of Countée Cullen*. Chicago: University of Chicago Press, 2012.

Turner, Darwin T. *In a Minor Chord: Three Afro-American Writers and Their Search for Identity*. Carbondale, IL: Southern Illinois University Press, 1971.

WEBSITES

The Amistad Research Center
www.amistadresearchcenter.org
The Amistad Research Center focuses on research and scholarship on African-American history.

Modern American Poetry: Countee Cullen
www.english.illinois.edu/maps/poets/a_f/cullen/cullen.htm
Furnished by the University of Illinois at Urbana-Champaign, the Modern American Poetry website hosts a database of biographies and literary criticism for modern American poets.

PBS: The African Americans: Many Rivers to Cross
www.pbs.org/wnet/african-americans-many-rivers-to-cross
The official website for the PBS series *The African Americans: Many Rivers to Cross.* In the series, Harvard professor Henry Louis Gates Jr. explores the history of African Americans from enslavement to modern times.

Poetry Foundation
www.poetryfoundation.org
The Poetry Foundation website contains critical essays and biographies on poets, as well as some of their poetry.

BIBLIOGRAPHY

Arden, Eugene. "The Early Harlem Novel." *Phylon* 20, no. 1 (1st Qtr., 1959): 25–31.

Baker, Houston A. Jr. *A Many-Colored Coat of Dreams: The Poetry of Countee Cullen*. Broadside Critics Series. Detroit, MI: Broadside Press, 1974.

Beckman, Wendy Hart. *Artists and Writers of the Harlem Renaissance*. Collective Biographies. Berkley Heights, NJ: Enslow Publishers, 2002.

Bland, Edward. "Racial Bias and Negro Poetry." *Poetry* 63, no. 6 (March 1944): 328–333.

Bontemps, Arna. "The Two Harlems." *American Scholar* 14, no. 2 (Spring 1945): 167–173.

Brown, Jericho. "How Not to Interview Black People about Police Brutality." *Harriet: A Poetry Blog*. April 30, 2015. Accessed September 1, 2015. http://www.poetryfoundation.org/harriet/2015/04/how-not-to-interview-black-people-about-police-brutality.

Brown, Lloyd W. "The West Indian as an Ethnic Stereotype in Black American Literature." *Negro American Literature Forum* 5, no. 1 (Spring, 1971): 8–14.

Brown, Sterling A. "The American Race Problem as Reflected in American Literature." *Journal of Negro Education* 8, no. 3 (July 1939): 275–290.

Brown, W. O. "The Nature of Race Consciousness." *Social Forces* 10, no. 1 (October 1931): 90–97.

Cleaves, Irene I. "The negro—a Lincoln Birthday Exercise." *Francis W. Parker School Year Book* 2 (June, 1913): 170–177.

Collier, Eugenia W. "I Do Not Marvel, Countee Cullen." In *Modern Black Poets: A Collection of Critical Essays*, edited by Donald B. Gibson, 69–83. Englewood Cliffs. NJ: Prentice Hall, 1973.

Corti, Lillian. "Countée Cullen's Medea." *African American Review* 32, no. 4 (Winter 1998): 621–634.

Dillon, George H. "Mr. Cullen's First Book." *Poetry* 28, no. 1 (1926): 50–53.

Dodson, Owen. "Countee Cullen (1903-1946)." *Phylon* 7, no. 1 (1st Qtr., 1946): 19–20.

Du Bois, Yolande. Letter from Yolande Du Bois to W. E. B. Du Bois, May 23, 1929. University of Massachusetts Amherst Libraries, 1929.

Early, Gerald, ed. *My Soul's High Song: The Collected Writings of Countee Cullen, Voice of the Harlem Renaissance*. New York: Doubleday, 1991.

Ferguson, Blanche E. *Countee Cullen and the Negro Renaissance*. New York: Dodd, Mead & Company, 1966.

Ferguson, Elizabeth A. "Race Consciousness among American Negroes." *Journal of Negro Education* 7, no. 1 (Jan., 1938): 32–40.

Fleming, Robert E. Review of *Countee Cullen* by Alan R. Shucard. *Black American Literature Forum* 19, no. 3 (Autumn, 1985): 129–130.

Ford, Nick Aaron. "A Blueprint for Negro Authors." *Phylon* 11, no. 4 (4th Qtr., 1950): 374–377.

Harper, Phillip Brian. "Passing for what? Racial Masquerade and the Demands of Upward Mobility." *Callaloo* 21, no. 2 (Spring 1998): 381–397.

Hart, Robert C. "Black-White Literary Relations in the Harlem Renaissance." *American Literature* 44, no. 4 (January 1973): 612–628.

Haskins, Jim. *The Harlem Renaissance*. Brookfield, CT: The Millbrook Press, 1996.

Haynes, George Edmund. "Changing Racial Attitudes and Customs." *Phylon* 2, no. 1 (1st Qtr., 1941): 28–43.

Jackson, Major, ed. *Countee Cullen: Collected Poems*. New York: Library of America, 2013.

James, Bertha Ten Eyck. "On the Danger Line." *Poetry* 35, no. 5 (February 1930): 286–289.

Jordan, June. "The Black Poet Speaks of Poetry: A Column: Essay and Review of Countee Cullen's Anthology, *Caroling Dusk*." *American Poetry Review* 3, no. 3 (1974): 49–51.

Locke, Alain. "A Critical Retrospect of the Literature of the Negro for 1947." *Phylon* 9, no. 1 (1st Qtr., 1948): 3–12.

———. "The Negro in Art." *Christian Education* 15, no. 2 (November 1931): 98–103.

———. "The Negro's Contribution to American Art and Literature." *Annals of the American Academy of Political and Social Science* 140 (November 1928): 234–247.

Molesworth, Charles. *And Bid Him Sing: A Biography of Countée Cullen*. Chicago: University of Chicago Press, 2012.

Paschal, Andrew G. "The Paradox of Negro Progress." *The Journal of Negro History* 16, no. 3 (July 1931): 251–265.

Sperry, Margaret. "Countee P. Cullen, Negro Boy Poet, Tells His Story." *Brooklyn Daily Eagle*, February 10, 1924.

Standing, T. G. "The Possibility of a Distinctive Culture Contribution from the American Negro." *Social Forces* 17, no. 1 (October 1938): 99–106.

Stokes, Mason. "There is Heterosexuality: Jessie Fauset, W. E. B. Du Bois, and the Problem of Desire." *African American Review* 44, no. 1/2 (Spring/Summer, 2011): 67–83.

Tindall, George Brown, and David Emory Shi. *America: A Narrative History*. 7th ed. Vol. 2. New York: W.W. Norton & Company, 2007.

Turner, Darwin T. *In a Minor Chord: Three Afro-American Writers and Their Search for Identity*. Carbondale, IL: Southern Illinois University Press, 1971.

Webster, Harvey Curtis. "A Difficult Career." *Poetry* 70, no. 4 (July 1947): 222–225.

Woodruff, Bertram L. "The Poetic Philosophy of Countee Cullen." *Phylon* 1, no. 3 (3rd Qtr., 1940): 213–223.

Woodson, C. G. Review of *To Make a Black Poet* by J. Saunders Redding.*0* 24, no. 3 (July 1939): 356–357.

INDEX

Page numbers in **boldface** are illustrations. Entries in **boldface** are glossary terms.

Rana Tahir holds a master of fine arts degree in writing from Pacific University in Forest Grove, Oregon. She has previously worked at Smithsonian Books as an editorial intern. Occasionally, she writes blogs about politics and poetry, and she is very active on Twitter. She lives in Portland, Oregon, with her loving husband, Will.